M.

vol. 2

The Molehill: Volume Two

Published with care and diligence by:
Rabbit Room Press
523 Heather Place
Nashville, Tennessee 37204
info@rabbitroom.com

Edited by A. S. Peterson
Cover concept, illustration, & design by C. Stewart (cstewartstudio.com)

Caution: Ingestion of this book may cause instances of great and terrible insight (not to mention great and terrible indigestion).

ISBN 978-0-9889632-1-4
First Edition
Printed in the United States of America
13 14 15 16 17 18— 6 5 4 3 2 1

RABBIT ROOM
PRESS

the MOLEHILL

volume 2

e collibus montes

Contents

Why is *The Molehill*?

by A. S. Peterson, Editor

"What is *The Molehill*?"

People ask me the question all the time. I usually tell them it's the Rabbit Room's literary journal, and then I find myself wanting to apologize for calling it something as highfalutin as "literary." But at the very least it's a bound collection of writing that aspires to literature. So maybe the question I really want to answer is this: "*Why* is *The Molehill*?" Why this when the literary world is already filled with more fine journals than most of us have time to read? Good question.

Early this year I sent an email to the Rabbit Room contributors inviting them to submit work for this second volume. Over the following months, their stories, poems, essays, and illustrations began trickling into my inbox. I'd read through each one, I'd talk it over with the writer and we'd decide whether it was the right piece, and then we'd begin editorial work—which is as much like a WWF match as anything you are likely to encounter in an email. There were a few pieces that didn't make the cut, and I was sad about each one of those, but what I found in the process was that two things were happening.

First, our small community was being drawn closer together. The Rabbit Room office stands at a sort of Nashville lunchtime nexus where, on any given day, just about anyone can walk through the door to say hello. Often Russ Ramsey stops in to chew the fat, or Jonathan Rogers camps out and grades papers, or Eric Peters parks himself in a corner to write songs. And more often than not, these unannounced drop-ins lead to conversations between friends about a *Molehill* piece, or a new album, or a new book. But the conversations run through deeper territories as well, wastelands of personal struggle, sin, and heartache. Little by little, the tiny connections made at this noonday crossroads produce real fruit, namely accountability and encouragement, both in creativity and in day-to-day life.

It's hard to create in a vacuum. So when a friend asks about your work, that vacuum is filled for a time and hopefully the creative act gets a little easier. That's one of the things I've appreciated about working on this volume. It hasn't been made in a vacuum. It's been assembled in the life-giving air of a community of writers and artists who know one another, trust one another, and are willing to give their time not only to *The Molehill*, but to their fellow men and women.

Second, we were sharpening each other. If I were to submit an essay to a contest or a magazine (or another literary journal), I'd do my best to write it well, and then I'd send it off to be judged by a nameless committee that would either accept or reject it for reasons I'd most likely never know. *The Molehill* contributors, however, know me (the editor) and they know one another, and that changes the game. There's a bit of amiable rivalry. Some feel they want to up their game to match Jonathan Rogers's "Flintknapper" or Andrew Peterson's poetry. Others are anxious to experiment in new methods and media. There's a feeling that we're all in this together and no one wants to be left behind. There's a sense of fun, of play, of creating for the sake of creation. And as a result, I think we write a little better, we edit a little longer, and we dig a little deeper into the creative mine in search of the rare gem worth the work of polishing. Those are good, healthy things for a writer when practiced in the midst of a gracious community.

I'm proud of each of the writers involved, proud of their work, and proud to call them my friends. In addition to a lot of familiar names from last year (including Walter Wangerin, Jr.), we've invited a few new folks along for the fun—gifted writers like Jeffrey Overstreet and Rebecca Reynolds as well as illustrators Jonny Jimison and Zach Franzen. The works of *Volume 2* range from a cartoon about pride and stubbornness, to poems that—like Jacob—wrestle with God, to the strange shores of a Georgia swamp where an alligator and an "angel" contend for the soul of a drunkard. There's no overarching theme, but for the perceptive reader, trends will certainly emerge, trends such as familial remembrance, the tension of creativity, and the extravagance of grace; they are by turns universal and personal, painful and joyful, abstract and plain as the day.

Through the shared work of editing and revision, all of the pieces in this collection have been changed, some of them drastically. And that's what community is all about. Change. We change one another, sharpen one another, hopefully for the better, and sometimes drastically. We learn to trust one another, to see with clearer eyes, to speak with wiser tongues, to write with deeper insight. Within community we become better versions of ourselves, and that goes for craft as well as for character. *The Molehill* is not a collection of works solicited from disparate literary sources. *The Molehill* is a gathering of the works of a unique, living community—a community whose members are invested in the refining of one another.

So why *is The Molehill*? Here's my answer: It *is* because we need each other. It *is* because the writers who contribute to it lean on one another for encouragement, for accountability, and for friendship. And they also need you, dear reader, because the act of creation isn't finished until the creation itself is given away. I don't know, but I like to think that in some mysterious way only the Spirit can know, maybe you need them as well, and through these tenuous connections between us, we are all, by grace, a community *in via* to a better version of itself.

E collibus montes. Amen.

A. S. Peterson
Editor, *The Molehill*

vol. 2

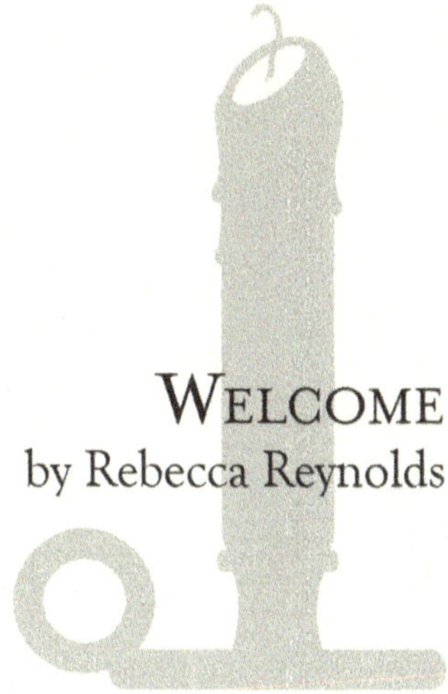

Welcome
by Rebecca Reynolds

Welcome to the precipice of truth.
Take one step off this edge,
and you will either fly
or you will perish.

I think, though,
what is most likely
is that you will first perish,
and then you will fly.

Or you can stay where you are,
stuck to that flat illusion of safety,
where you will simply coagulate
into a denser version
of what has already bored you to death,
bound you to death,
driven you here,
until you stand staring over the edge,
into certain loss
and hope afire.

pleethe: *v.* to beg for teeth

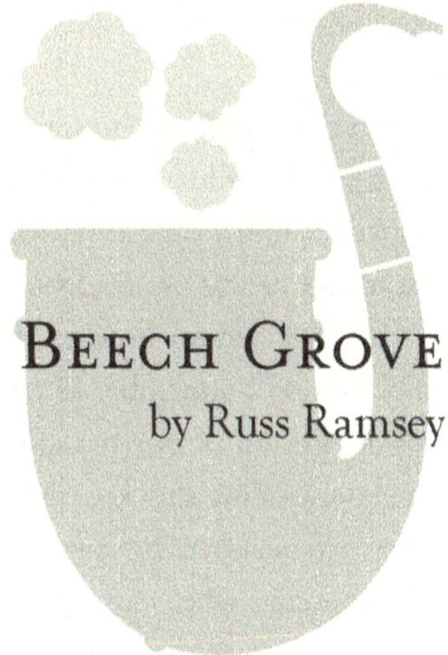

Beech Grove

by Russ Ramsey

In the fields of central Indiana, at the intersection of an old gravel road and the highway that divides the county down the middle, stands Beech Grove School, the old brick one-room schoolhouse my grandfather attended as a boy. Inside, a detective kneels in front of a busted safe, carefully brushing on a thin layer of fingerprint dust in the hope that he might be able to piece together what exactly happened there. He shakes his head as he looks around the room. "I sure am sorry," he tells us. "Someone really made a mess of your place, didn't they?" He doesn't know the half of it.

I was four when dad moved our family to Tipton, a small town built by farming and industry. Where the railways and county roads converged, speculators built factories, stockyards, and grain cribs—attracting people who understood that making a living there would not happen overnight. Building a life in such a place took years and it required everything a family had to give, so people put down roots. They birthed the coming generations in their living rooms and buried their dead in the cemeteries they carved out from among the fields they farmed. Families with names like Ripberger, Tragesser, Tebbe, and Schmidt had been around so long that a boy growing up there imagined those last names were as common to the world as Jones or Smith.

My grandfather on my father's side sold us an acre right next to his house, square in the middle of his property. Living next to him meant we lived with him because he spent as much time as he could outdoors, gardening and caring for his land, and that meant he was always around.

He included my brother and me in his work. He was the first person to pay us for our labor. I remember as vividly as anything the day my brother, who had been outside, ran up to our living room window and slapped a five-dollar bill against the glass, looking shocked and overjoyed as though he had fallen into unexpected riches. I remember thinking he looked older. Neither of us ever had that kind of money, except when our grandparents from New England would send us a little something in our birthday cards.

"Where did you get that?" I asked.

"Grandpa told me to pick up sticks in the yard beside the barn so he could mow. He gave it to me when I finished," he said.

This new wrinkle of being paid so handsomely for such simple work unlocked a world of possibility in our minds. I put on my shoes and ran over to see if there was anything I could do for my grandfather. He looked as though he half expected my visit and I ended that day with five dollars of my own. We were kings that day, my brother and I.

I loved my grandfather for including us when we were boys, and I loved him for the way he was committed to making us into men. When we worked with him in his garden, he made sure we did things just the way he wanted. He also made us understand that this was not open for debate. He believed there were jobs for men and jobs for boys. When we first started working with him—when we were "all boy, no man"—he would only take us one at a time because, as he used to say, "One boy's a boy, two boys is half a boy, three boys is no boy at all."

In time, as we proved ourselves, he began to include us in the work of men. Few things made our hearts soar more than when Grandpa put one of his tools in our hands and let us work beside him, and few things brought us a deeper sense of satisfaction than when he paid us after the work was finished. Boys don't get paid. Men get paid.

But the truth was we were boys, and my grandfather's land was a little boy's dream. Buck Creek cut right through the fields and woods I had memorized so well. The creek was alive with crawdads, catfish, and turtles. And though I had never seen one, I had heard Buck Creek was also home to its share of cottonmouth water moccasins. People said that one strike could kill a boy. Dead. The serpents hid in the rushes, we imagined, coiled with aggression, venom sealed behind their hollow fangs, eager for release. The danger drew us to the banks and the closer we got to where we imagined they were hiding, the more we felt like men.

A grass-covered tractor lane led from the northern edge of my grandfather's property into a stand of trees we referred to simply as "the woods." At the far end of the woods, an old shed with a dirt floor and a tin roof rested against an old red oak. The shed and tree looked like a couple of old friends holding each other up. Time had woven the branches, eaves, and rafters together until the two had become inseparable. That shed was an excellent bunker for a boy with a cap gun to hole up in and blast his way through the Bolivian soldiers who had finally gotten the drop on old Butch and Sundance. I rescued many maidens in those woods, and I got the drop on a lot of bad guys too.

At the other end of the tractor lane, across the yard from Grandpa's house, stood a one hundred-year-old barn with a loft full of hay bales, rusty tools, and feral cats. Time and neglect had begun to pull at its walls and weaken its floors. Between the possibility of getting lockjaw from a rusty nail or the floorboards giving way underfoot, that old barn was even more dangerous than the cottonmouths. Like a snake, it could poison our blood, but it could also break our bones.

My brother and I were forbidden to go into that barn, which made it one of our favorite places in the world. We'd sneak in through a side door, out of the line of sight of Grandpa's living room window, climb up the old plank ladder into the loft and stack the hay bales like giant blocks to create a maze of secret rooms and tunnels.

Occasionally my grandfather would suspect I was in there. How, I don't know. But sometimes he would slide open that heavy door, step into the center aisle, and study the stalls, tack room, and loft, listening. He'd call out, "Anyone here?"

I'd watch from the rafters, still as a statue.

"Hello?" He called out again.

His mind held a collection of images of the ways things were supposed to look—the proper latching of a door, the glistening of a full water trough, the motes of dust hanging like stars between him and clean lines of the hayloft. I knew the combination of his failing eyesight and the dust between us would hide me so long as I didn't move. His eyes would trust the stillness and his memory would fill in the details of what he couldn't see. There we'd be, me in the place of my trespass, him seeing but not perceiving, my present sins hidden from him as surely as those of his past were locked away from me.

"Anyone here, I say?"

My grandfather slid the old door closed and fastened the latch, locking me inside my private world. Though I was too young to understand, I was doing something then that I have done with every relationship I've known since. I was trying to manage what my grandfather could see of me. I wanted him to see the helpful boy who walked beside his mower picking up black walnuts to protect the blade, but not the boy who stole the half empty pouches of chewing tobacco off his kitchen counter when he wasn't home. I wanted him to see me standing at his back door, hoping to tag along when he went to the diner for lunch, but not the boy hiding in plain sight behind the ladder he was now too old to climb.

I had to have been one of the more familiar figures in my grandfather's world. I was his grandson and his next-door neighbor. We saw each other every day. I worked at his side. But his old eyes had grown too dim to convince him that the object behind the ladder up in the haymow was me, his own flesh and blood. I was Jacob hidden in the texture and scent of Esau, fooling the old man who, though he clearly remained skeptical, had no choice but to accept that my stillness and silence meant I wasn't there.

What we show of ourselves to others is what they will come to know of us, of who we are. Hiding there in plain sight, so familiar and yet so unrecognizable, felt like a transgression. It wasn't just that I shouldn't have hidden from my grandfather; there shouldn't have existed in me the instinct to do so in the first place. But there it was. This was the first time I remember feeling guilt, and the feeling came with a companion as old as guilt itself—the impulse to hide. I was only a child. What had I to hide?

The landscape of my boyhood was marked out in my memory by that barn, a creek, the woods, and the old schoolhouse standing alone at the end of our dirt road. My home was a collection of details, relief, history, and memories all tied together into a country I had come to know by heart. I can close my eyes and see it. I imagine this is how it is for anyone who spent his younger years in one place. I came to know my home not as a single place, but as a network of places connected to each other.

But now when I return to that place, it is not as I remember. Dirt roads have been paved, old buildings have been knocked down, and new ones have been built in their places. Entire neighborhoods have cropped up where only corn once grew.

But the land I had known so well as a boy, the place so new to me and undiscovered, was also the land of my grandfather's old age and it had changed quite a bit since the days of his youth. The schoolhouse he attended, Beech Grove School, took its name because it was built in front of an orchard of beech trees—a landmark dotting the flat, Indiana horizon. People could see it from miles away. Common sense had chosen the school's name before a single brick was laid, just as it had chosen names for Cave Spring Road or Brick Church Lane.

The reasons behind names like these, when they are first given, are obvious. They are part of the observable world. But over time, things change—the brick church gets destroyed in a fire, the cave spring dries up, the beech trees die off, and so do the generations who named them. There was a time when that stand of trees sheltered the school from the prairie winds, but I have no memory of it. When my grandfather went there, the school was cooled in the afternoon sun under the shade of those trees. Perhaps one or two of them were good climbing trees, giving the children a natural playground. Maybe some of them had young lover's initials carved into the bark, with a heart and an arrow surrounding the letters. I don't know. Those trees were not part of the landscape I knew. But for one, they were all gone, and the one that did remain was itself mostly dead.

My grandfather was an elegant man. Whether he was in the garden in his straw hat, green work pants and white button-down shirt, or headed off to work at the Chrysler dealership in his suit and cuff links, smelling of pomade and Old Spice, he was always put together, modest, and neat as a pin.

He belonged to a generation that cared about the appearance of things—about order and design—so every year or two he would hand my parents a few twenty-dollar bills, neatly folded together, and tell them, "A boy needs a suit."

This was a liturgical act, a ritual with a purpose. My grandfather gave my parents this money so that we would have something to wear to his funeral, when that day came. He was not a sickly man, but he was a pragmatist. He knew his day would come, and he knew with every passing hour that it was inching closer. Since he lived by the sweat of his brow, he had no intention of wasting his twilight years in a hospital bed. He figured one summer day he would stand up after weeding a row of beans, his heart would give out, and that would be that.

"A boy needs a suit," he said. "You just never know."

Our mother would take my brother and me to the local department store where we would try on various combinations of slacks, sport coats, and clip-on ties until we each had something both we and our mother could live with. I don't remember when the phrase took hold, but everyone in our family came to know these outfits as our "funeral clothes." We understood these were ceremonial garments—vestments we'd put on when the time came for us boys to gain our earliest lessons in mortality and grief. Grandpa imagined there would come a day when our parents would have to tell us that he had died, and though we wouldn't understand all that meant, we would at least know what to do next. We'd put on our funeral clothes.

Besides this primary purpose, there was another ceremony we observed in these garments—this on the very day we brought them home. When we got back from the store, my brother and I would put them on and pose for a Polaroid in the yard with our dog Zombie, whom my grandfather loved as dearly as he had ever loved anything. Then, still dressed up, Zombie at our side, we would take the picture to over to grandpa's house. He would look us up and down for a minute and then study the picture in silence as we waited. In that tiny image he could see us as we would be, standing beside his casket. It seemed to please him to know we were at least in some way outfitted to let him take his leave from us, and maybe to help him one last time. Perhaps he imagined himself lying in repose as a line of friends and family filed past to get one last look at him while my brother and I stood as a people prepared, shaking the mourners' hands and offering words of comfort. Or maybe he just wanted us to look nice when we buried our own faces into our parents' sides, weeping our own tears over this confusing introduction to death.

After looking at the picture for a while, he'd say, "Those are fine boys. Fine boys." It was a kind of benediction. With that blessing, we would hurry home to get out of those clothes, unclipping our ties as we ran.

A year or two would pass and we'd do it all over again.

In its early years, the Beech Grove School was the only place for miles where the migrant workers and farmers could send their children for a proper education. Eventually industry took hold in the area and the little town got organized. They built a courthouse, a post office, a hospital, a bank, and a new school closer to the center of things. The old schoolhouse stayed empty until a handful of faithful families converted it into a little church, which struggled along but somehow managed to survive under one name or another all the way up until the late 1980s. When the church at last closed its doors, the schoolhouse stood vacant until my father leased it as an office for his computer business.

Sometime around midnight on Christmas Day of 1994, while I was home from college, shadowy figures kicked in the front door of the old schoolhouse and looted my father's new office. The next morning, a neighbor phoned to ask my dad if he knew the schoolhouse door was standing wide open. Dad called the police and a detective met us there.

The detective studied the sanctuary and shook his head. The place looked like a scene from a movie, like a room torn apart by secret operatives searching for clandestine files. Loose paper, upended furniture, cables, tools, and old machine parts lay scattered across the room. The door to the safe lay on the floor beside the strongbox, bent and empty.

The detective said, "Why do people do these things? I sure am sorry. Someone really made a mess of your place, didn't they? And on Christmas too."

A rush of anxiety came over me. I was keeping a secret. I worried that if the detective were to turn his questions on me, I would fold, guilty as a bandit, because I knew something he did not, something relevant to his investigation, something I did not want to tell him. What he didn't know was that the papers and upended furniture strewn across the room were actually just as they had been before the burglars arrived. Yes, thieves kicked in the door and cracked the safe, but the mess they walked into was all our own, and we had been working on it for a long time.

My father's computer business had been dying for several years. It was a tough industry in a tough town, and dad had all but resigned himself to the fact that he couldn't keep it going much longer. The move from an office in town to the old schoolhouse was a step along the way to dissolving the business he'd spent the better part of two decades building. Now years of cables, machines, parts, and office supplies lay scattered throughout the building with no apparent order to anyone but my father.

After the detective left, dad and I began the slow work of seeing what, if anything, was lost. We were in good spirits, really. It was Christmas, after all. A new year was just around the corner. We talked as we worked. We talked about the years when his business was in the center of town and how I used to walk to his office after school to wait for him to take me home. We talked about when he took the whole family to a Lake Tahoe casino for a conference about operating systems. He played the slots and won a souvenir cup full of quarters, then sent my brother and me to the arcade to kill an afternoon. We talked about the short but story-filled list of past employees. I was on that list. He talked about how much his industry had changed, how much I'd grown and how it was more of a relief than anything to know he was moving on.

I never considered that schoolhouse mine—not in the way I did Grandpa's barn or Buck Creek. Its windows were frosted white and set too high in the walls to see through from the ground. Until my dad signed his lease, I had never even seen the inside of it. Not once. Growing up I knew the outside of that schoolhouse as well as anyone, but I could no more tell you what was contained within those walls than I could describe the interior vaults of Fort Knox. It wasn't until the burglars broke open the safe and the detective started his investigation and told us to take an inventory of what had been lost that I ever felt I had any place at all in that building. It had been as unknown to me as it was familiar. And in that sense, as I was about to find out, it was a lot like my grandfather.

Late that afternoon the phone rang. It was a doctor from the nursing home where my grandfather had been living for the past year. Dad listened on the line for a minute, said, "Okay," and then hung up.

He said, "Doctor says we probably ought to get down there."

I arrived at the hospital about fifteen minutes after my father. I remember that day with vivid clarity. I walked into my grandfather's room and saw my dad standing on the far side, facing me. Between us, my grandfather lay motionless in his bed. My father was looking at me with tears in his eyes and a slight smile at the corners of his mouth.

My grandfather looked almost unrecognizable—gaunt, ashen, waxy, and so very still.

"He just left us," my father said. "Not more than five minutes ago. I was here. I held his hand. I told him it was okay to go."

Tears gathered and clung to my father's lower eyelids so that when he blinked, they all fell to the floor at the same time. He straightened his father's hair with his hand.

"He took in a deep breath and let it out real slow, and then he was gone," he said.

Neither of us said anything for a while after that. I prayed. I sensed the presence of God there with us. My father, though stunned with grief and shock, seemed genuinely thankful for the peaceful, painless way my grandfather had died, and he counted it a holy honor to have been there to tell him it was okay to go.

I remember how still everything became in that room—how the air seemed to take on a sepia tone and how I sensed that the moment we were living was ancient, set for us before the foundation of the world. Three generations of fathers and sons gathered in a room, one now gone and two preparing to sift through the rubble of what remained.

"You're going to need a suit," my father said.

The world is a place of order and design.

Long ago, God told his people to make sure they taught their sons and daughters about him. When they tucked their children in for the night, when they walked with them along the road, when they gathered to eat, they were to talk about the Lord and his promises. God said, "Tell your children what I've told you. Bind my words to your minds and hearts, and to theirs." And this is just what they did. They tied Torah-filled tefellin boxes to their foreheads and wrote scripture on the doorposts of their homes and gates, so that in all their comings and goings, their minds—young and old alike—would be filled with ancient truth.

God wanted his people to tell their children about him so that they might know him, but he wasn't speaking of something that only worked in matters of faith. He was telling us how he had designed the world itself to work. What a father gives his son is what that boy will know. It is who he'll become. It is this way for all of us. Nobody gets out clean. This is part of the order of creation.

What my grandfather had given me was what I knew of him. And the era in which he had given it was my context for knowing; it was the era of my first twenty years and of his last. He had given me so much and I loved him for it—he the priest over countless rites of passage that marked my boyhood, me the acolyte learning how to absorb the wisdom of the aged.

Of course I only knew a fraction of my grandfather's story. The first fifty years of his life were all but unknown to me, except for a few historical details. But there in that hospital room it was as though someone had kicked in the doors of his private world and my father and I were about to begin sifting through the secret sanctuary of his greatest moments and deepest sins—that place so familiar and so unknown—to account for what we lost that day.

In the weeks that followed, my father began to tell me some of my grandfather's stories from before I was born. They were layered with broken promises, the sowing of more than his share of wild oats, and hurt. As it turned out, when he was younger he was a hard man to know and an even harder man to love. I had no idea of the messes he left in his wake—messes that shaped my father, messes that are still shaping me, messes even my own children catch a glimpse of every so often.

My father told me stories from his own life too—accounts of where he had been most deeply wounded and of his struggle to connect with his own sons because of how little he had to go on from his father. My grandfather, the man I knew, was not the man my father had known when he was my age. I didn't know how sad parts of my grandfather's life had been. I only knew him as an old man who had already experienced most of the loss he would face in life. Heartache and time had taken a hard man and made him gentle. That's the man I knew.

My father didn't tell me these stories out of anger or spite, but out of grief and hope—hope that they were well on their way to becoming old tales. As he told them, I was struck by a thought I had never considered: my grandfather had a life before I was born—and if that was true, my mother and father must have too, lives that were rich, complex, and virtually unknown to me. Another thought stormed in behind that one: if this was true, then all three of them must have had rich, complex lives virtually unknown to me even as I lived with them.

Who was I, after all? I wasn't the center of their lives. I was important to them, and loved. But neither my grandfather nor my parents sought to make sure I was intimately acquainted with the inner workings of their hearts. How could they convey such a thing? How could I bear it? Sometimes, even when we're standing right in front of each other, we lack too much information to really see each other. Of course we don't want it to be this way, but what else can we do?

I see the detective with his investigation kit, surveying the room looking for clues to trace out the narrative of what took place. But all that remains for him are the traces of a story he will never be able to put back together. He tells us it's pretty rare that they actually recover any stolen property.

Time claims so much.

I remember "Beech Grove School" engraved in the capstone over the entrance in a simple but elegant font. I see my grandfather standing at the steps, books and homework under his arm. I remember what it was like to be thirteen and I imagine my grandfather and the other boys playing and fighting behind the grove of beech trees, settling the questions that boys of that age need to settle. I see huddles of girls whispering and giggling in a private language the boys will never learn. I see the teacher with the most basic tools of her trade—something to write with, something to write on, and something with which to instill fear and keep order.

I see children as children are and have always been—innocent, curious, mischievous, and moldable. They blend together into a single thing, a social order gathered on a proving ground, wondering who they are, where they fit, what they'll become. They are a class like any other class. I can see my grandfather in his seat amid the other freckled boys and pony-tailed girls working their numbers on their chalkboards.

Three o'clock comes and I see them filter out into the yard. They walk home, some to their mothers' kisses. Others to a father's criticism. Some have love poured into them. Others have it driven out. Some don't have a care in the world. Others carry unimaginable burdens—the creeping advance of a sickness for which there is no cure, the longing to be close to a parent but thwarted by an addiction that stands between them like a demon with a flaming sword—the child still in the garden of hope but the parent somewhere east of Eden.

My grandfather carries in his bag a tin canister of pencils and crayons and a cigar box of hand-bound composition books filled with drawings of dissected frogs and the anatomies of flowers. I can see these items in particular because these are relics I actually found one day while rummaging through some old boxes he kept in one of his outbuildings. I hid them in one of my secret rooms in the hayloft, one near the rafters by the window. I'd return often to those brittle, yellowed pages, neatly printed in a child's hand; one thirteen-year-old boy looking over the shoulder of another, sixty years after the fact. The flowers he had drawn had long since withered, but the sketches and words he wrote about them remained as true as ever because this world is a place of order and design. Grass withers and flowers fade, but the word of truth stands forever. In this case, the truth Grandpa's frogs and flowers were telling me was that he was a boy once, and no matter how familiar he might have been to me, there were entire epochs of his life that I knew nothing about, and never would, except for what those few relics revealed and the few images my mind suggested. And except for what carried over in the messes he left behind.

I was a teenager when the last remaining beech tree blew down in a storm. It was the only one I had ever seen on the schoolhouse property. I remember how it lay behind the building like the fallen dead with no one to carry off its remains. I remember how the seasons stripped it of its bark and how it lay there bone white, burying itself into the earth until the last opaque memories of how Beech Grove School got its name faded away forever.

That tree is long gone now. So is my grandfather. Someday I will join their number as one whose memory will be preserved by others. Will they praise me saying that I gave them a sense of security in the same way that stately grove in its fruitful years assured the community around it that they were home? Or will they remember only my sins and tell of some great, ruinous fall? If my story turns out anything like my grandfather's they will have plenty to draw on from either end of that continuum. The day is coming when those close to me will hold the remnants of my story like relics in a cigar box. On that day I will forfeit the ability to direct the narrative. And the story they tell with the bits they've kept will be all of my story that remains. What a sacred responsibility we have in this telling of old tales.

That school house, Grandpa's barn, the woods—they're all different now. I try to tell my children about them, but I know that what they imagine is not what actually was. If we are going to remember, we must fight to remember. As we remember, we will remember people. We will remember them not as they were, but as they were to us. In doing this we will judge their lives according to a limited stack of evidence, unfamiliar with all that was kept locked away from our sight. We must admit that we see through a glass darkly and that much of what there is to know is, like that grove of beech trees, lost. And what we do know, we know only in part. For this, there must be grace.

THE FARMER

by Rebecca Reynolds

I would have driven eight hours
just to listen to him pray.

When supper is set, I try to stand near him,
because he smells like the fields,
like the Burley that hangs to dry in the barn,
like potatoes packed away in the cool of his root cellar,
like hard white soap,
and like wild onions.

His shirts are worn thin from time and economy.
You would think he was a shy man,
unless you were patient.
Then he would tell you all the secrets of growing things.

He cultivates the tiger melon because it is fragrant.
He cultivates the beans and the corn.
He has learned to can, dry, cure, and forgive,
because he has known scarcity.

He has knelt in drought and asked for rain,
knelt over children dying,
knelt over graves and births.
He has hid himself in the Rock of Ages,
keeping small enough to become great.

The simple life is not a simple thing.
To walk one's span of days
watching the deconstruction of the world,
holding fast to the first, best things—
it is more than I have done.
But he has spent his morning hours
under the clear, violet skies,
and he has spent his summer evenings
bowing over boiled greens,
thanking God for the bounty.

I have seen him shut his eyes before
that tinny old piano at the country Baptist church
while it rang out visions of high heaven.
His countenance was like the face of Moses.

It is one thing to speak of grace, and another to live it out
among twelve red chickens and twelve black cows
in the same house where you came to love
the wife of your youth
while she faded and you learned to make the meals
and wipe the edges of her mouth
and remind her which of your boys
had gone already to Jesus.

In that same house turns a circle
where the farmer collects his fallen children
and the fallen they have collected themselves.
I have gathered with them,
holding his hand while he talked to our Father.
He pressed my palm with a shaking thumb,
intent beyond walls and fields,
intent unto glory.

spive: *n.* a dwelling of clandestine bees

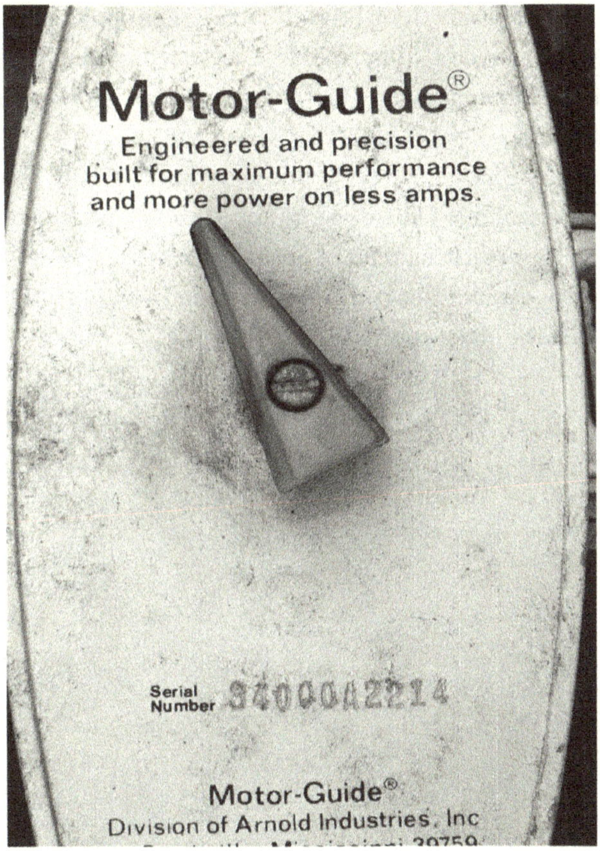

Trolling Motor

by Eric Peters

As did the fishing, the act of reading in his beat-to-hell, twelve-foot aluminum bateau brought him singular pleasure. Having witnessed the very same eccentricity in his father, it became the son's habit to stuff a novel inside the battery box where it could stay dry during the long float through duckweed and lilies. When the fish stopped biting, rather than retreat to the launch, he'd plunge a homemade concrete anchor into the depths or tie off beneath a tupelo, and open a tepid cola and a can of Vienna sausages. There, deep within the black, meandering veins of Bayou Sorrel, he read aloud various Pulitzer and Man Booker Prize-winners to the curious ears of the Atchafalaya watershed.

There was nothing haughty in the act, no elitist need to civilize the backwoods; he merely liked the sound of Dillard against the feathery backdrop of bald cypress, felt at ease in the reverberating echo of Stegner skimming across the water. As a child his father brought him along on fishing trips, and now, judging by the ensuing silence of the fauna, he understood why.

The Ancient Paths

by Andrew Peterson

My father was born a century too late.

He has no moustache—just a white beard that frames his jaw like a chinstrap. He's not Amish. He's not a Civil War reenactment buff. He just likes to wear a beard that's terrifically uncool. He smokes a pipe and knows the name of every bird on the feeder. He's a preacher—not just a pastor, or a minister, but a *preacher.* What I grew up listening to was preaching, complete with the pacing and the flecks of spittle that popped out from between his lips like tiny grenades. He raised his voice and waved his arms, then whispered and pleaded, and just when you weren't expecting it he raised his voice again. He preached every week, Sunday morning and Sunday night—two different sermons—which makes a solid 104 sermons a year. By the time I graduated high school and joined my first band I had heard my dad proclaim the Gospel almost 2,000 times, and that's not including Wednesday night Bible study.

But there's one sermon I remember best.

The year after graduation he preached at the community homecoming celebration down at the football field. Half the town showed up, so the bleachers were filled with a beautiful mixture of denomination and race. Only at football games had I ever seen that many black people and white people sitting together. Women wore bonnets, men wore ties, and they all fanned their faces with their bulletins, a mighty chorus of flapping paper. My father wore a black, old-timey suit with a ribbon tie. He even wore one of those old flat-rimmed hats that parsons sported a century ago. If he'd had his way, I'm sure he would have galloped up to the podium on a horse, as if he'd ridden in from the revival circuit just in time for the service. He was in his element. I was excited to see him in such a setting, because there were African-Americans in the audience, and *they* knew how to listen to a sermon. Every "amen" and "glory be" was fuel thrown on the fire. Their affirmations bolstered my father's confidence and gave his sentences rhythm and poetry. He became more than he was.

The refrain of the sermon was "Give me that old time religion!" and when I say "refrain," I mean it. Like the sermons and stump speeches of old, he delivered lines about the faith of our fathers and mothers, then sang (though he isn't a singer) "Give me that *old* time religion." Then he praised the early church of Acts, and how they had everything in common and more people were added to their number daily, and he said, "Give me that *old* time re-*ligion*." He preached the white people out of their self-consciousness and Southern-fried propriety and by the end of the sermon the Baptists and the Church of Christ folks and the Methodists and the six people who attended the little Church of God in Christ were nodding and muttering, "That's right, praise be," and "Thank you, Jesus," not about religion—which wasn't his point—but about the old ways. The Ancient Paths. The sermon was a call to the misty reaches of the days of yore, to the streets of Jerusalem and its outlying villages where news of Jesus' resurrection spread like a new spring bubbling down a mountain, to a time when Peter's vision of the animals in the sheet convinced him that all people—*all* people—were welcome at the banqueting table.

I was proud of my dad that day. I loved watching him strut the stage. I loved how he doggedly repeated that chorus, waving his arms like he just might flap into the air and swoop over the stands like a mad bird while the little old ladies clutched their giant purses and the weathered farmers dove for cover. "Give me that old time religion," he cawed. And he wore them down. Until at last, they sang along. They got it. They knew that he wasn't saying the old ways are better just because they're old. He wasn't condemning the next generation just because it was new. He was saying that people are broken; it has been thus since Eden and will be until the great New Eden is established for ever and ever, world without end. So go back, back to when the earth was young and God walked in the garden, and Adam and Eve followed in his footsteps like toddlers learning to walk. *Those* were the good old days, those and none other. So hold on to that which matters. Pay no mind to the whims of culture, but walk in the ways of the Ancient of Days. The grass withers and the flowers fall, but the Word of the Lord endures forever. Amen.

When I go home to visit it always feels like I've stepped through a time portal. One minute I'm in the city—a Starbucks on every corner, free Wi-Fi, fast cars, flat screens, self-checkout lanes—and the next I'm standing by an old dry well under a mossy pecan tree. I hear chickens clucking. I remind myself to keep an eye out for rattlesnakes. My mom is in the garden wearing a flowery hat, yanking potatoes from the good earth, and my dad is in the wood shop with a pipe dangling from his mouth. Here, people still write checks at the grocery store. They chop wood. They come home from church meeting to discover bushels of fresh corn on the porch, a gift from the neighbor's farm.

I know it's not perfect. There's more sin in that little town than there is sweet tea, and that's saying something. But when I imagine an old world like the one they live in, and then I remove the sin, the anger, the pettiness, and the feuds that plague even the quaintest of quaint little towns, I have a pretty good idea of what Heaven will be like. I imagine a place where the footpaths are older than the dinosaurs, where our lives are so long the seeds we plant seem to sprout and blossom overnight, and where love, that timeless power that beats in the heart of God, leads our every step.

I don't remember how that sermon ended. I stood beside the bleachers, having just come home from my first real tour, and looked on arrogantly, a young man who had been to the upper Midwest and was therefore wise in ways that these quaint townspeople couldn't possibly grasp. But by the time my dad had finished, I was stirred by what had played out on that flatbed stage. Imagine it: one man in period dress, shouting at the top of his lungs with the fool's hope that a few of the words flying out at the crowd might burrow deep and hold fast enough to actually effect change. Dad was sweaty and quivering with hope when, to raucous applause, he descended the steps from the makeshift stage like a rockstar. For probably the first and only time in his life, he reminded me of Springsteen. He gave them what they wanted, which in that moment was also exactly what they needed. It was what I needed too, though I didn't realize it then.

Someone told me once that the Christian journey leads inevitably to orthodoxy, which to my thinking means that the way of Jesus weaves itself through the mountainous ages, forward in time and glory but backward in direction, to the very gates of Eden. It was to that garden my father bid us make haste, where we shall slough off the burden of the curse and enter. Perhaps we'll find the great city isn't so different from that small town—at least as it was on that hot summer day on the football field. I hope the angels give him a horse to ride, because I believe he will travel those fair lands for eternity, a circuit rider of old, trumpeting not the Kingdom to come, but the Kingdom that came.

> *"This is what the LORD says: 'Stand at the crossroads and look; ask for the ancient paths, ask where the good way is, and walk in it, and you will find rest for your souls.'"*
> —Jeremiah 6:16, NIV

Then Sings My Soul:
A Summons to Play Without Ceasing
by Jeffrey Overstreet

He kept the door closed when he worked, as if to protect a secret. "It's the room where the stories come from," he explained.

Year after year, I heard the patter of his keyboard run past midnight in our upstairs bedroom. He'd write all weekend too. He had the boundless ambition of a five-year-old and the feverish concentration of a juggler with twelve fiery batons in the air.

To live in the kingdom of play—for a time, that was his ambition. He descended into story as if into a mine, and returned glowing for what he found.

Submit his manuscripts to publishers? He rarely showed any interest, even after college. He was pessimistic about publishing, cringed at talk of self-promotion, and tossed aside guides for finding agents as if they were manuals for playing the lottery. He had taken to heart the counsel of his college writing advisor: Beware of graduate writing programs. "You have such a love for writing," she said. "I worry that the fiercely competitive nature of grad school would crush the passion you have for play."

It's hard to believe that his imagination could run out of stories. But I don't think he's been here for a while. I no longer hear the pacing, the typing, the conversations between characters, the film scores shaking the walls. Last time I saw a pen in his hand, he seemed anxious, with shadows like bruises under his eyes, new creases in his brow.

It's just a phase, I've been telling myself. He'll be back. Inspiration is seasonal. He'll write Chapter One of a new story soon.

But today, my worries win. I stop at his closed door. The face of Jim Henson stares back at me from an old Apple Computers poster that the writer pinned there. "Think Different," says the Apple slogan.

I listen, knock. Nothing. I go inside.

It's a nutshell of a room—two steps deep, three steps wide, and cluttered. When I raise the shade, sunlight finds dust and cobwebs. But for the wind wheezing at the window, it's quiet as a pharaoh's tomb.

The room is crowded with souvenirs that he sometimes calls "talismans," "muses," "icons."

One wall is busy with movie posters, another with framed album covers—records that served as storytelling soundtracks. Photographs freeze wild landscapes from his travels in Ireland and Wales, thumbtacked to a corkboard alongside tickets from memorable concerts. The burdened bookshelves bend. A host of figurines pose on the edges, like the droids from *Star Wars*, two- and three-inches tall, their details thumb-worn from decades of play.

His writing desk—a puppet stage that his grandfather built for him when he was very young—has three walls and a window cut in the front that frames a stage-shelf. As a boy, he performed puppet shows on that stage for friends and neighbors. In recent years, on the very same stage, characters were born in Moleskine journals and on a laptop computer. A cup full of pens, a half-burned candlestick, and a mug with a bag of old Earl Grey like some empty insect's cocoon. 64 crayons burn in an open box, bright as birthday candles.

On the floor around his chair, books by Dr. Seuss, A.A. Milne, Bill Peet, and other favorite childhood authors mingle with those written by giants from his teen and young adult years—Norton Juster, Michael Ende, Madeleine L'Engle, J. R. R. Tolkien, Mark Helprin, Marilynne Robinson, Cormac McCarthy—as if he's been searching them for a half-remembered storyline.

Puppets stare blankly into space. There's Kermit the Frog, smiling as always. The writer saved his allowance when he was only seven years old for the joy of bringing this character to life.

"Icons." That seems right. This haunted silence makes the room feel like a closet in a chapel.

I open the turntable, and there's the vinyl on the spindle—one of the soundtracks that once summoned him into storytelling. I guide the tone arm, set the needle down, and wince. It's that famously motivational theme to *Chariots of Fire*. He must have been desperate for inspiration. I suppose it could have been worse—it could have been "Eye of the Tiger."

"Nostalgia is death," Bob Dylan told *The Los Angeles Times* in 1992. Wisdom from an artist who never ceases from his play. Still, when we find ourselves stuck at a dead end, perhaps it's necessary to look back, to figure out where we took a wrong turn, where we lost that golden thread.

I sit down at the puppet-stage desk and look out at a blustery, blue-skied autumn afternoon. The window frames a scene of crows at play. They're flinging themselves from a telephone pole up into the wind, testing their abilities, learning how to negotiate gusts of Seattle weather. Stunt-pilots of dizzying agility, they aren't thinking about who might be watching. They are doing this for the love of the game.

If I'm going to be any help to our resident writer, I suspect I'll find what I need right here.

While we are meant to "put away childish things," surely we are not meant to lose that sense of play that kindled our ambitions. Shouldn't it grow up with us—the inclination to immerse ourselves in play's fierce concentration?

It began for him, as for most of us, in infancy, with an ambition to find something lost.

As a child in his mother's arms, he gazed intently into her face, learning to recognize her eyes, her smile, her voice. In her presence, he was safe, nourished, loved. Home. He answered her delight with smiles and laughter.

One day, Mother covered her face with the curtain of her hands, or a blanket's edge, or a magazine cover. Her features vanished. All was lost. He searched the void, but could not find the pattern.

"Where'd she go?" Mother's voice asked. *I don't know*, he thought. *I can't find her*. Fear clutched his chest, and his arms thrashed in alarm. Could this be the end of the world?

Then, she dropped the curtain. "Here I am!"

And the child, in a rush of recognition and relief, laughed for joy. Order was restored. She hadn't forsaken him; she was there all along.

But then, she did it again. The fear returned at once. What if she was gone for good this time? What had ended well before might not end well a second time. "Where's Mom?" came the voice. "I don't know!" he wanted to shout. But there—her face, revealed again. Recognition. Reunion. Relief.

And, most importantly, trust. The beginnings of faith. He found an "assurance of things hoped for, a conviction of things not seen."

This excitement was addictive. He soon sought new forms of play—momentary disruption, spine-tingling tension, and then the gratifying thrill of resolution.

And so it goes. To calm their infants, fathers dance their babies' feet in the air and sing a rhythmic song. On airplanes, mothers quell their child's wailing by pulling toys from their purses. At suppertime, unwanted utensils become airplanes descending. Play quiets the scream, captivates, provides a space in which faith can flourish.

The boy rattled the bars of his crib in the early morning tension, demanding what was missing. Emboldened, he climbed out of jail one day and crawled through the house—to strive, to seek, to find what made the world whole. Play had inspired him to resolve tensions on his own.

He would soon turn the tables—hide himself beneath a tablecloth, jump out to surprise his mother. In time, he would leap from high apple-tree boughs just for the fleeting thrill of falling with the assurance that the soft ground would catch him.

In the same spirit, he was drawn to story.

When Mother and Father were busy, and the long waits for their attention wrung out his patience, his interest in stuffed animals increased. Those faces were not his parents' faces. They would not respond, say reassuring things, and hug him back—unless he imagined that they did.

And so he gave them names and voices. He afflicted them with crises, frights, and anxieties based on tensions he had experienced or imagined. In this way, he reminded himself that dissonance would resolve, that fears could be overcome.

Such childhood charades become, for all of us, an early rehearsal for the rest of our lives.

Everywhere, every day, faith is tested in countless ways. Crises complicate work, home, and traffic. Headlines declare that a criminal has not been found, a disease is spreading, a storm looms fearsome on the radar, a dictator vows nuclear devastation. Feeling pangs of distress, dizzy spells, we fumble for a sense of meaning or design. We seek comfort in the love of friends and family, the reassuring and remedial beauty of nature, the liturgy of worship, the mysteries of art.

Where the news alarms with endless trouble, art invites us through trouble to a moment of insight about either the world or, perhaps, the artist's understanding of it. Music brings rhythm and grace to a chaotic commute. A mystery novel provides a superficial sense of justice, or a sitcom a feeling of domestic chaos resolved, before the lamp's turned off for the night. A Friday night popcorn movie does the same for a week full of tedium.

Some, in zealous pursuit of revelation and consolation, become artists. And for a time, the boy sought satisfaction by writing stories in which his heroes resolved their crises by cleverness and force. It felt good to awaken monsters and then smash them, to imagine he could right the wrong world.

This compulsion began when he was only five. Opening a newspaper, he was startled by an advertisement for Steven Spielberg's movie *Jaws*—a shark rushing up toward a vulnerable swimmer. His insides turned to jelly.

So he anxiously sketched himself a picture book. A swimmer turns to face a predator and strikes it in the eye with a sword. Already, he liked believing that he could save the world.

This storytelling posture was reinforced at church, where he observed that plots could be "tools" used to deliver a message about who wins and who loses. He would write to show Jesus as a hero and believers as a winning team, treating other characters as Problems to Be Solved, Villains to Overcome. Those who did not conform went up in punishing flames.

Thus he wrote with more aggression than play, the pen proving equal to the sword. But the stories were formulaic, moralistic, unimaginative. They fed the ego instead of the soul.

By contrast, the public library seemed like a wonderland of surprises. He found himself drawn out of the Children's corner and into aisles labeled "Literature." These larger books were like his father's—they didn't have illustrations. He felt grown up turning the pages of greater imaginations, playing in a larger and seemingly dangerous world. These stories drew him into the experiences of others beyond his community, where the world was not so predictable, not so easily divided into "us" and "them."

He had not yet read Frederick Buechner, who would someday explain to him, "'The world speaks of the holy in the only language it knows, which is a worldly language."

In these foreign countries, he was moved by flawed and failing characters. He sometimes felt unsettling sympathies for villains.

What is more, there was something about his favorites that he could not easily duplicate. A mystery moved through the pages like mist, a poetic quality more enchanting than the simple moral tales of Sunday School.

And though he may not have noticed the shift, a new ambition had begun to take hold, one nobler than the compulsion to lash out at what frightened him. He wanted a sense of mystery and majesty in his own stories, to be swept up in the play of something more magnificent than a "message." He did not want to force a conclusion he had already imagined.

He wanted to be surprised.

The needle gets my attention, *tap-tap-tapping* the end of *Chariots of Fire* Side One.

It's coming back to me now—this movie opened just as the boy, only eleven years old, was producing one story of aggression and defeat after another. I think I can see how it gave him a license to play.

Endorsed by his fellow churchgoers, *Chariots of Fire* showed a Christian—Eric Liddell, a famous Scotsman who served as a missionary in China—preaching the Gospel, ministering to a congregation, taking a stand for God's law, and then earning Olympic glory. His medals were celebrated as God's blessing upon him for his righteousness. It was a happy ending sure to satisfy evangelicals. And when it won the Oscar for Best Picture, the young writer was caught up in a sort of euphoria, as if God had scored a major victory.

But despite the sermon illustrations, it was not the virtuous believer's Olympic glory that most influenced him.

The film's most fervent evangelical figure, Jenny, Eric's sister, voices frustration when Eric postpones missionary work so he can run in the Olympics. Shouldn't his highest priority be the salvation of Chinese souls? By comparison, running seems self-indulgent.

But Eric does not divide his life into "ministry" and running. He says, "I believe God made me for a purpose, but he also made me fast. And when I run I feel His pleasure."

To feel God's pleasure. That, thought the young writer, *is what I feel when wind fills the sails of a story. That is what I feel when I'm at play. When I'm finding out instead of forcing matters to a particular end.*

Unselfconscious, caught up, enthralled, Liddell ran wildly, a holy fool in track shoes, his head thrown back in a spiritual ecstasy. Yes, he won victories, but they were never the reason for the running. It was as though he found a state of perfection mid-stride, opening himself like a satellite dish to glory. And when Eric's father told him, "You can glorify God by peeling a potato if you peel it to perfection," perhaps the young writer felt permission to focus on characters, paragraphs, and punctuation instead of proselytizing. After all, the "Flying Scotsman's" perfection attracted attention instead of demanding it. Liddell *became* a living testimony instead of *declaring* one.

On the writer's desk, I find a photocopied page from a Thomas Merton journal: "If you write for God, you will reach many men and bring them joy. If you write for men, you may make some money, and you may give someone a little joy, and you may make a noise in the world—for a little while. If you write only for yourself, you can read what you yourself have written, and after ten minutes, you will be so disgusted you will wish that you were dead."

You won't find any track shoes in our writer's closet. He does have a basketball, but it's down in the basement. As a child, he loved to practice, to hone his skills. There was a particular thrill in running a play with skill and grace, in making a three-point shot under pressure, in the scramble of players pursuing a loose ball and then charging to the hoop.

But as his high school teammates and coaches increased in their ambition for championships, the pressure to win drained his enjoyment. He quit the team so he could have more time for storytelling, so he could "lose himself" without fear of losing.

In those years, the young writer's work took a different turn. He began to strive for excellence rather than argument, poetry more than pronouncement. He found pleasure in wordplay, in the suggestiveness of things. More and more, he found surprises on his own pages. Through high school and college, he wrote stacks of stories, often exploring territories that were dark and strange, delighted by what he found there. After late night hours of immersion, he would surface with the glow of someone who has just returned from a mountaintop or the Grand Canyon, exhilarated.

His ambition was now to play without ceasing—to investigate mysteries, cast imaginative nets, and catch ideas too wild for any paraphrase. He flung himself into the wind, testing his feathers and his flight.

Here's another thumbtacked quotation, this one from Chesterton, pinned to this puppet stage frame: "There is one thing that gives radiance to everything. It is the idea of something around the corner."

It was this sense of something around the corner that compelled him to escape into a story when hard times came.

They came suddenly, the week of his college graduation, in the form of an excruciating betrayal and loss. His marriage of two years ended for reasons that struck him as hard, as fast, and as unexpectedly as a red-light runner. The lies he discovered had come from a loss of faith. Despite his fumbling attempts to save the relationship, it was too late.

To escape hourly attacks of anger, grief, and despair, he plunged into story. Composing other worlds with a new desperation, he followed characters into shadowy realms in search of consolation. One idea after another collapsed. The plots seemed too easy, their resolutions unpersuasive. But he continued.

In two years' time, he found his way into a story in which a thief robs a kingdom of its colors, and a heartbroken prince goes in search of revelation. That world held his attention for more than a decade.

Right here, in this small room, he struggled with his questions, weary but refusing to give up, begging for a blessing. And in doing so, he found a path not around but through the darkness—for his characters, and for himself. His wandering prince found peace not by vanquishing an enemy, not by rebuilding what he'd lost, but by following a mystery that captivated his imagination, even when it seemed foolish to go on.

Thus, a child's daily practice of play became the work by which a man's faith was rekindled. And it was the fruit of this feverish play that, ten years and a dozen rewrites later, turned his world upside down. A benevolent stranger appeared one day, read an excerpt of his work, and put him in touch with a publisher.

A few months later, three book contracts arrived within a few days of each other.

Long nights of writing grew longer. Weekends were marathons run on a laptop, and he threw back mugs of coffee the way runners grab paper cups of water from the sidelines. Two more contracts arrived within a year.

The attention was gratifying, sure. An editor's enthusiasm or a good review could brighten a dreary Seattle sky. He made new friends and found opportunities to meet many artists who had inspired him. Yes, it changed his life.

Coworkers, friends at church, family members, and readers approached him saying, "Wow, it must be a dream come true!" or "You must feel like you won the lottery!" He responded politely. But we could see those cynical furrows deepening in his brow. He wouldn't complain. Publication was a blessing, right? Hadn't his life been a prayer? And wasn't this was the grand answer, a blessing he had not dared to desire?

But as he pursued deadlines over four years, his posture changed again. He spent lunch breaks, evenings, Saturdays, and Sundays hard at work on rewrites and revisions, his mind on meeting expectations. Marketing endeavors, speaking engagements, readings and book-signings, social networking. He stopped exercising, gained weight, lost sleep. He turned down so many invitations, even long-standing friendships began to dry up.

Once that fifth book was published, we had grown accustomed to his absence. He works now in cafés and pubs and city parks, looking for ways to keep his head above the surface of the stress. He's not one of the fortunate few who can quit their day jobs to "just write." His future looks like one of endless striving. He's a plant uprooted, deprived of water, sunlight, nourishment. He finds encouragement in readers' responses, but compliments are a fleeting thrill. Play has become production, and exploration . . . obligation.

Perhaps you remember the night in March 1999 when Italian film director Roberto Benigni, that irrepressible clown, won his Oscar for *Life is Beautiful*, a movie of spectacular comic invention. In his joyous acceptance speech, Begnini said, "I would like to thank my parents in Vergaio, in a little village in Italy. They gave me their biggest gift, their poverty, and I want to thank them for the lesson of my life."

The audience laughed when Begnini said this. But our writer blinked back tears, recalling days when he had worked quickly and easily, without comparison or competition, his storylines spreading like blackberry vines.

The world of new media offers the writer so many incredible ways to connect with his audience, such easy access to inspiring art and entertainment, and so many new ways to "get the work in front of people." But new media counteracts contemplation in its desperation to hold our attention. And the hard work of using it to get attention is a powerfully addictive pursuit. It can come to dominate our attention even as it whispers that what we are doing is for the good of our work and for the good of the world. As it takes hold, it slowly corrupts any capacity for contemplation and creativity.

In *Chariots of Fire*, there was another story told—one about a fiercely competitive runner named Harold Abrahams who lost an important race when he turned, mid-stride, to check other runners' progress. Similarly, our writer has lost his own stride in striving to maximize sales, to gain attention and succeed. Feedback, reviews, and statistics can be informative, but nothing spoils creative unselfconsciousness like a preoccupation with how others have "rated," "liked," or "disliked" your work.

Still, competition has become the frame through which our culture views every creative pursuit. Television has moved from programs about culinary art to programs about cooking competitions. The art of cinema is reduced to a race for the Oscars, and the music hailed as "Best" is determined largely by popularity and fashion. Ambitious young talents are packaged for potential "Idol" status, sparking talk about style rather than substance. Even the news is fraught with split-screen shouting matches that prompt us to pick a side.

This process pollutes our experience of so many good things, and it distorts our ambitions. Scholars are increasingly convinced that a lack of play can lead to depression and even suicidal impulses.

The writer now feels an urgency every time he lifts a pen. The fear of losing momentum, of being forgotten, is poisonous. He's lost the unselfconscious joys that kindled within him the ambition to run, to write, to play.

Again, that rhythmic spark—the needle bumping the paper circle at the record's center.

As I lift the tone arm, I seem to hear a sigh, a suggestion from the motor and the rotating circle. "Disengage."

This box of crayons on his desk—it arrived in the mail last year.

Our resident writer, riding a wave of unexpected attention, had recently spoken about storytelling at a New York conference for artists. As an image of his six-year-old self at play lit up a big screen, he spoke of those early compulsions to write, draw, and role-play.

"I wanted the box of 64 crayons," he told them. "Never got it."

And then they heard a catch in his throat. He departed the script and said, "It was all play, you see. No one had used the word 'art' to me, and I wish they wouldn't. No one asked me if I was 'an artist,' and I wish they never would. I think art is a verdict. I think we should still be playing."

It was just an ad-lib, but the audience cheered. "They weren't cheering for me," he admitted, reflecting on that moment. "They were calling out to people they hadn't seen in many years. They were cheering for a spirit they'd once known."

And soon after that lecture appeared online, this box of 64 appeared in the mail—a gift from someone he had never met. Her name was Claire. She'd seen the video and, weary of her own challenges, she shared that longing for play.

"I need to pay attention to this," he said. "To think more about why we forget." But I'm sure what he meant was something more personal, more urgent. It sounded like a cry for help.

Play is always possible. It doesn't take much. With only pencils, paper, and an old typewriter, our resident writer once lost himself for hours, for days, and returned with treasure. Jim Henson changed the world with a dream and this friendly green puppet, a toy he made by clipping his grandmother's coat. Handel famously locked himself in a room and when he emerged, he carried the music of *The Messiah*.

There's an old Sufi saying: "New organs of perception come into being as a result of necessity. Therefore, O Man, increase your necessity, so that you may increase your perception."

On the writing desk, Kermit is smiling as always. Shuffling through the writer's LPs, I find one that is even older than *Chariots of Fire*, a soundtrack from the days when the boy first wrote stories. The needle plucks a banjo, and the notes ring out like a curse-breaking spell.

Although the writer learned to appreciate Bach concertos and Beethoven anthems, and although he sings along with every song that the Beatles and Bono ever sang, these notes—the beginning of "The Rainbow Connection"—inspire him like nothing else ever composed.

Some will say he's nostalgic, preoccupied with childish things. No, it's more than that. Like the bells that once called the people of a town to Mass, it summons him to that state of receptivity, that openness to revelation. The lyrics turn his attention outward, toward what the heavens declare.

I sing along.

Have you been half asleep, and have you heard voices?
I've heard them calling my name.
Is this the sweet sound that calls the young sailors?
The voice might be one and the same.
I've heard it too many times to ignore it.
It's something that I'm supposed to be . . .

These words seem to have been written for a nine-year-old boy who yearned to discover his place in the world. But they also spoke to a young man who felt a summons to explore, to practice his art, to pursue something true.

They speak to me too. I am a weary, middle-aged man who barely recognizes himself anymore. That boy, that young man, that writer who found faith through play—they were each me, of course.

And this song is reuniting and reconciling us.

Madeleine L'Engle, writing about her enduring affection for children's stories, insisted that her age was not an isolated chronological statistic, but only the most recent addition of a year to her life: "I am also four, and twelve, and fifteen, and twenty-three, and thirty-one, and forty-five and . . . and . . . and . . ." It feels like freedom, to be all of those things at once.

I was startled when the audience attending my New York lecture sang all the way through the chorus. So many kindred spirits—"all of us watching and wishing we'd find it." And I came home longing to hear "the sweet sound" calling my name again. I lost track of it somewhere. I turned my gaze away from the source of my inspiration.

What is the posture of a man who writes for God? "The fear of the Lord," we're told, "is the beginning of wisdom." That fear is not horror, but reverential awe and wonder. We're drawn further up, further in. If we shake, it's with the resonance of bells rung.

Souls do not sing on command; souls sing because they cannot help themselves.

Beauty—in nature and in art—rings those bells. I might be dumbstruck in the Georgia O'Keeffe Museum, or lost in the shoreline fog of a Puget Sound morning. I might be singing in the crowd at a concert, or taking pictures of bones bleached white by the sun outside of Santa Fe, New Mexico. In those moments, I am a child smiling back into my Maker's face.

The Scriptures insist, again and again, that when we are in a state of faith, no matter our maturity, we are like children at play. In Proverbs 8, Wisdom plays like a child, creating the world. The Leviathan, in Psalm 104, plays—and God enjoys it. Isaiah 11 promises that a child in God's kingdom will play fearlessly beside a snake's nest. In Zecharaiah 8's picture of the kingdom, "Boys and girls will fill the streets with their games."

Maybe the answer for me is in this: Even Kermit, in that whimsical Hollywood story, became burdened by anxiety and wandered away from the campfire, hanging his head. But one of his companions gazed up into a sky full of California stars, and said, "You could get lost in a sky like that." Then he did. In this posture of star-gazing awe, his soul began to sing. "I've never been there, but I know the way," he sings. "I'm going to go back there someday."

It can happen to any of us. Even when the world around us roils in seeming disarray, if we have eyes to see, we might suddenly behold him, the one who loves us and completes us. "The soul should always stand ajar," wrote Emily Dickinson. She knew a thing or two about posture.

I lift the needle from the record. Perhaps this room is not a tomb after all. Not yet. But I've spent enough time looking back. These souvenirs are not the answer. They are only signposts, pointing me in the right direction.

It's time to answer God's invitation to play.

I think I'll drive down to the edge of the ocean at twilight. I love the way that water can catch and hold the daylight after dusk, as if clinging to a memory so that it's easier to believe in the coming dawn.

If I go down there and, like e. e. cummings, thank my God for "most this amazing day," perhaps "the eyes of my eyes" will open. I might forget myself and become a witness again, catching light and, perhaps, reflecting it.

O Lord my God, when I in awesome wonder
Consider all the worlds thy hands have made
I see the stars, I hear the rolling thunder
Thy power throughout the universe displayed.

Then sings my soul.

spudgeon: *v.* to beat soundly with a potato

Tea with Beasts

by S. D. Smith
with Illustrations by Zach Franzen

Are you frightened of animals, those four-feeted beasts,
Who bite us and scratch us and have us for feasts?

I'm with you, for certain, I'm sometimes afraid,
But one thing can alter my mind once it's made.

Do you know what makes all the difference to me?
Well, I'll tell you! It's whether the beast enjoys tea.

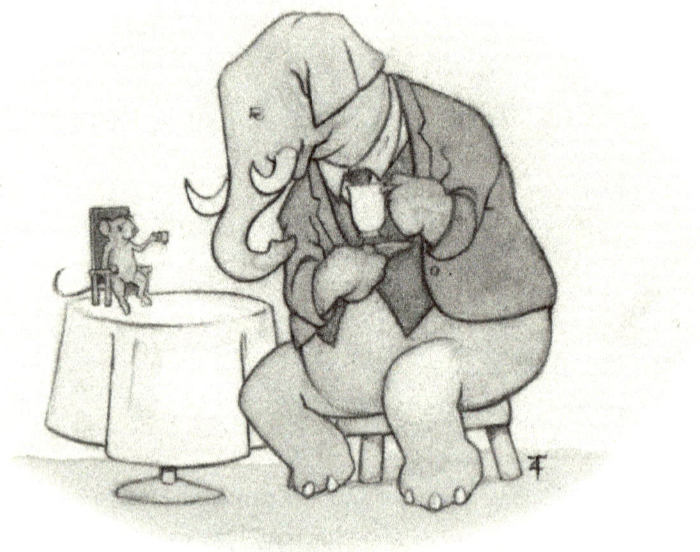

Oh, tea makes an enemy into a friend.
When you sit 'round the table, old rifts start to mend.

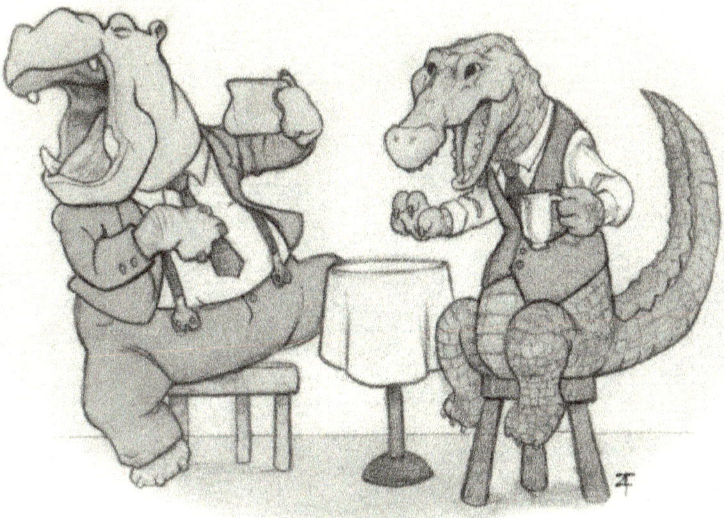

"I'm terribly sorry for biting your aunt!"
"Think no more of it, my friend, for I shan't."

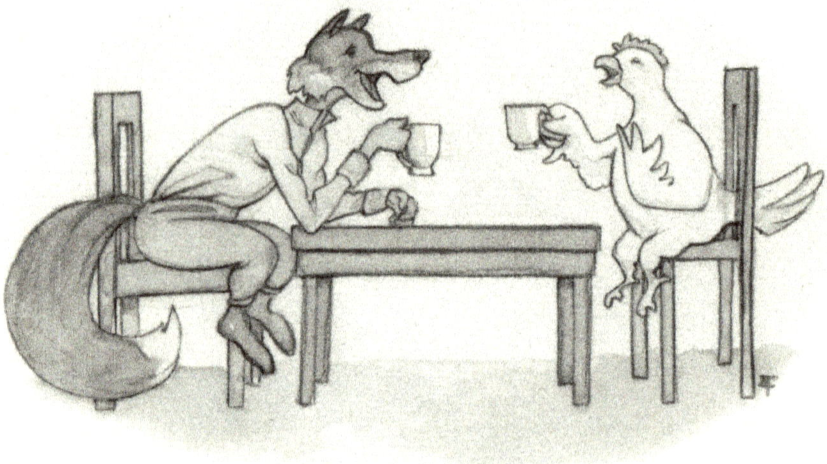

"That business when I had your school chum for lunch?"
"No worries," says rabbit while biscuits are munched.

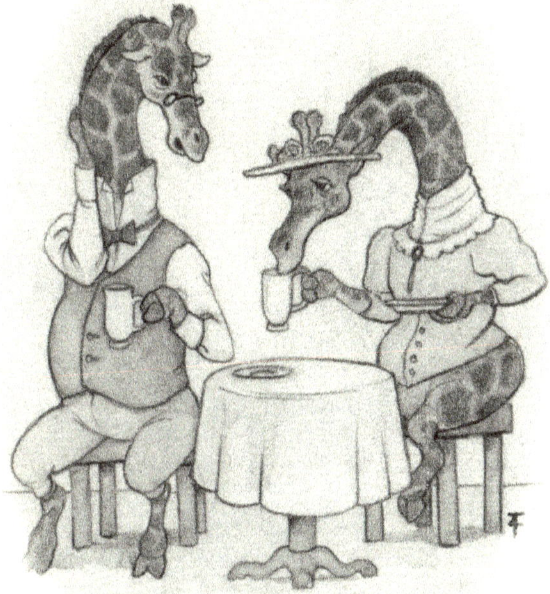

The former ill feelings, you ask where they went?
Well, we're all more polite with a British accent.

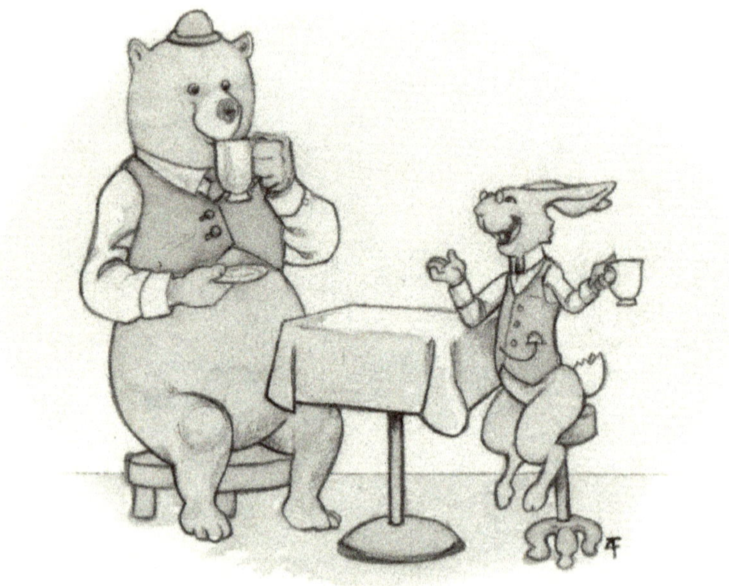

And whoever can think of revenge when he sees,
A bear dressed and civil and sipping on tea?

A Cask of Golden Ale

by Walter Wangerin, Jr.

Rang, rung, ringing,
My story is beginning.

—The First Part—

Chapter One

Once upon a time, when kings ruled England and the New World too, a young apprentice sat beside his master on the wooden steps of a wooden porch. It was a soft summer's evening. Together they gazed into the golden sunset. The apprentice heaved a sad sigh then raised a tankard to his lips and drank. The old man likewise drank from his own tankard. They were savoring the best ale that they had made that year.

This was supposed to be a celebration, because the apprentice had finally learned all that his master had to teach him, and he was about to go out into the wide world to earn a living on his own.

The old man was a brewmaster, the finest brewmaster in all the land between the eastern coast and the western mountains. For three years he had trained the apprentice in the craft of making ale, had shown the lad his secrets, and had blessed him with an old man's wisdom. During those three years, each had come to love the other as grandfathers and grandsons love.

Now in the twilight and in the silence the brewmaster felt pride and sorrow, both. His apprentice would soon be as good a brewer as he, and then would be the best in the land—that for pride. At the same time, he was losing his best beloved—that for sorrow.

And the lad felt fear and sorrow and mournfulness too. To go out into strange territories scared him. To leave the old man saddened him. But because the old man was afflicted with a serious illness in his chest—well, that grieved him.

The old master took out an ancient clay pipe, and stuffed it with tobacco, and lit it, and took long pulls, and puffed long puffs. Goodby, goodby.

CHAPTER TWO

The apprentice had been born the youngest of three brothers on a small farm in the New World. Their father plowed behind a pair of oxen. Their mother grew vegetables and patched pants.

Now, the older brothers were ne'er-do-wells. They chewed straws and slept in sunlight while all the chickens flew the coop. The youngest boy led the milk-cow to pasture, and led her home again, and washed her teats and milked her twice a day.

Their parents counted themselves blessed, for they had good work and good food and three sons to serve them when they'd grown too old to serve themselves. Moreover, when they crossed the sea from England to the New World, they brought with them three heirlooms which had been passed down from generation to generation—and would in time be passed on to their sons.

But then came the killing year.

A summer-long drought dried the land, and withered the crops, and yellowed the garden vegetables. High winds flattened the cow shed so that the cow ran off. Hailstorms crushed the coop and killed the chickens. And the creek bed hardened and cracked. And the well ran dry.

The good man killed one ox so that his family would have meat while he walked the other ox a long way to the nearest village. He went to sell the poor beast. He was gone a month. His wife and children became scarecrows. The two older boys complained and complained as if these evils were their parents' fault.

"And you!" they said to their brother. "You should run away for the good of us all. We'll have more to eat."

The good farmer came crawling back. Thieves had stolen his money and beaten him. After his good wife had laid him in their bed, he smiled as if he saw an angel.

Then he died, and they buried him in the hard, hard ground.

The mother of the three boys, stricken by her husband's death, lay down on the bed where he had lain. She called her sons.

"When you have buried me beside your father," she said, "look in the chiffo-robe." To the oldest son she said, "The bright silver buckle is yours." To the second son she said, "The silver ring is yours." And to the youngest: "Yours are the two gold doubloons. My dear ones," she said to them all, "make good lives for yourselves."

Late in the night of their mother's death, the older brothers whispered, "Two doubloons for that simpleton? Why, he doesn't know a penny from a puppet show."

The youngest boy was fourteen years old. What could he do when he woke in the morning? He could bury his mother tenderly. But then he could do nothing but travel westward through the tangled woods.

Chapter Three

So now the young apprentice turned to look at his master, who was puffing on an ancient clay pipe. "Sir," he pleaded with the man, "I have already lost one father. Why can't I stay here and take care of you in your old age?"

The old man felt a spear of pain pierce his lungs. He gritted his teeth but did not groan. Instead, he pretended to be cross. "What good are your skills if you stay secluded here? What good is your wisdom if you don't go out to use it yourself?"

The lad set his empty tankard on the wooden step and sighed. "If I must, I must."

"You must!" the old man scolded. Oh, it hurt him to scold his beloved boy. He got up and went inside and brought out a cask of the finest golden ale there ever was.

"Take this as my gift to you," he said. "Learn its secrets. Honor its powers, my grandson, and never, never sin with them."

But the lad, his grandson, was no fool. He knew the old man hoped to die alone.

—The Second Part—

Chapter Four

The next morning our lad rose up, and heaved the cask up and onto his shoulder (Goodby, goodby), and began to travel through the tangled woods.

He walked a long way. The farther he walked, the heavier grew his cask.

At midday the journeyman brewer come out of the dark woods into a meadow bright and buzzing and as hot as steam under the sun. Walking, still walking and bearing the heavy cask of golden ale, sweat popped out on the lad's brow and ran into his eyes.

He sat down on a tussock and said, "How can I lighten my load?"

Soon he saw a distinguished gentleman coming his way.

"That's how I'll lighten my load," said the lad. "I'll share some ale with that respectable fellow, and the cask will be less by two tankards."

By the look of him, the man was a scholar, tiny eyes behind Franklin bi-focals, a body pale and lean, a long black frock down his back. Two linen flaps were attached to the collar at his throat. On his head sat the broad-brimmed hat of a Puritan preacher.

"Good day," said the journeyman lad.

"Good indeed," answered the Puritan. "A day the Lord hath made!" He scrutinized the lad a while, then said, "What does a boy as pretty as you plan to do with the liquid treasure inside his cask?"

"Yes," said the lad, "it is the finest of treasures, brewed by the finest of men. I plan to share it with someone as fine and as wise as he."

"Well," said the Puritan all dressed in black, preparing to sit on another tussock, "you shan't find a finer, more worthy person than I."

"Well and good," said the journeyman, "and I hope it is true. But before we drink you must tell me who you are."

"Why, I am the Lord God himself!"

The lad closed his mouth and squinted in the sunlight, taking the measure of the Lord in his black frock and broad-brimmed hat. Then he said: "No, don't sit down, sir. I cannot share my ale with you, for you destroy hard-working farmers, the mothers and the fathers of the children—and you never give a reason why."

So the lad stood up and heaved the cask onto his shoulder and kept on walking, and the cask kept growing heavier and heavier until all his muscles ached and complained.

What then?

In the middle of the afternoon, the journeyman stumbled down a stony slope into a stony valley. There were paths everywhere he looked. They criss-crossed each other among a hundred boulders. They looked like wrinkles in an ancient face.

Wearily, he dropped onto a low stone and laid his burden down beside him.

Suddenly he saw a crooked fellow jump up like jack-in-the-box from behind one boulder, then fall and hide behind another. The lad heard such giddy laughter that it made him smile. Skinny as a whip, the crooked man bounded from path to path and rock to rock, always leaping closer to the journeyman lad—giggling, snorting, laughing.

"What fun!" thought the lad, feeling bubbles of joy in his tummy.

"Good day," he said, and he hopped up to the top of a house-sized boulder. He sat cross-legged and clapped his hands.

"Good for this," he answered, "and better for that. Now, my pretty, let's have a chat. You have a cask."

"I have a cask."

"What's in your cask?"

"Golden ale."

"Golden ale-co*hol*! you mean. *Ha ha!* A drink's a drunk however you cut it. Right? Now then, *hee hee*. What do you plan to do with your golden brew?"

"I plan to lighten my load by sharing it with someone as good and as wise as the brewmaster who brewed it," said the lad.

"I get and I give," cried the jubilant man. "I give and I get, get, get. *Woo-hoo!* You won't meet a shrewder buddy than me for a trick and a trade and a tankard."

"Well and good," said the journeyman, "and I hope it is so, for you make me laugh. But first, sir, you must tell me who you are."

"Why, Beetle-zee-bub! I'm Nick o' the tricks! Lucy of light, if you please. And to speak it plainly, I am the Devil!"

The lad took the measure of the Devil, skinny as a whip, rolling eyeballs, a tricky mouth, arms and legs all covered with colors.

Finally the lad said, "No, sir. I cannot share my ale with you, for you turn good into evil, you turn brothers against their brother, and souls from right to wrong, and hands from work to thievery."

Onward, then, and onward the poor lad staggered, while the cask swelled bigger and longer than his back from the nape of his neck to the back of his knees.

What then?

By twilight the journeyman brewer stopped at the bank of a river. He kneeled and splashed water on his face. When he stood again, lo: on a river-rock nearby sat a man who was dark enough to be his own shadow. The man watched as the lad wiped the wet from his face with his sleeve.

Tick, tick! Tick, tick! Across the shadow-man's waistcoat was a chain from which hung a clock as loud and as large as a railroad conductor's clock.

Though the lad was startled, he did not lose his good manners. "Good evening," he said.

"As are all evenings good," said the shadow-man, "for gently do they lay the days down on their beds, and then do call the owls to sing each dying day to sleep. But you, my comrade—here you stand unbedded and awake. I can, if you please, touch sweet sleep into your eyes."

"No, sir. No, sir, I must stand watch the whole night through."

"Such a task. Why?"

"I cannot leave my cask unattended."

The shadow-man gazed in moonlight at the enormous cask. "A very heavy burden, indeed," he said.

"If I could lighten the cask," said the lad, "I could lighten my task."

"Comrade, I would help you, if I could."

"Well. I want to find someone as honest and as wise as the man who brewed this golden ale. I want to share a healthy portion with such a someone."

"There is not," said the shadow-man, "a soul in the world with whom I would refuse to drink a tankard to the last draft and into oblivion."

"But before we drink, sir, you must tell me who you are."

"I am Death."

The journeyman peered at the man who seemed to blot out a thousand stars and to swallow up the moonlight.

Finally the lad said, "Yes, I will share my ale with you. You are a truth-teller. You don't play favorites, but treat everyone equally. And there is no one, neither man nor woman, who will not meet you at the end of their days."

So the lad sat down. He broached the cask, and the ale glugged cheerfully into their two tankards, and they drank all night in deep meditation, and the journeyman lad never drifted into sleep.

Shortly before dawn, when the sky was greyer than Death is grey, Death said, "I have never tasted ale so golden, nor met a youth with such good sense, nor found a comrade who was unafraid of me. Friend, I want to give you a gift. Do you know that it is I who control life because I control the end of life?"

"Yes," said the journeyman. "I know that you are the truth. Death can never lie."

"Well, then, I am filling your cask with a particular power. From now on it will be light and easy to carry. And its ale will never run dry. Listen," said Death. "A sip of your ale will cure the sick. When you enter the sickroom, look for me. If I am sitting at the foot of the bed, know that the golden ale will restore your patient to health and to life again. But if I am sitting at the head of the bed, the ale can do nothing. The patient will die."

And of course, no one in the sick-room would be able to see Death except his young and fearless comrade.

"You shall be a master Physician!"

A master Physician. Well, well, well.

Immediately the lad remembered the old brewmaster whom he'd left yesterday morning.

"Sir," he said, "Let me first go back and heal my grandfather."

But Death shook his head. "Even now," he said, "I am sitting at the head of the good man's bed. You have another master now."

—The Third Part—

Chapter Five

And so it was. The Master Physician's word was always true.

When he said, "I am so sorry; the deacon will die," the deacon died.

When he said, "Your daughter will live," the mother received her daughter with joy, and ran to tell her neighbors the news: "A sip of his ale was all it took!"

His fame spread everywhere in the New World and over the ocean and all the way to England.

The years passed.

One day two men came and begged the Physician for help, since they were sick unto death.

"I will pay you well," the first man said. "See? Here is my precious silver ring."

The second man said, "I can pay you better than that. Here is a bright silver buckle to hold up your pants."

"And besides these treasures," said the Master Physician, "I expect from each of you a gold doubloon."

"Oh, sir," they said nervously. "We spent our gold doubloons."

Well, well. Well, the Master Physician played no favorites. So the first man lived, and the second man died, and when the Doctor removed the dead man's pants, he kept the silver buckle.

And the years passed.

Chapter Six

Then the daughter of the King of England fell ill and lay down upon her bed.

The King's physicians were baffled and helpless. Daily the beautiful princess grew weaker. Her cheeks were flushed as red as roses. Her brow was as pale as alabaster.

She closed her eyes and didn't open them again.

The King sent his herald east and west, crying, "Who will heal my child before she leaves my poor heart cold and empty?"

The herald returned. "They say," he said, "that there is a Master Physician. . . ."

So the King commanded his fastest ships to sail to the New World. "If the man can heal my daughter, he shall have half my kingdom!"

Half the kingdom of a *King*?

Well, the Master Physician decided that it was time to be paid according to his importance. In no time at all, he came to the King's castle carrying his casket of golden ale. Servants led him up the stairs to the princess in her bed. When he entered the sick-room, he saw the King in purple raiment and the Queen with diamonds in her hair and philosophers and maids in rows—and the poor child scarcely breathing. And Death.

Death was sitting on a chair at the head of the bed.

The Master Physician was about to speak the awful news, when he noticed that Death was dozing! Death's head had drooped, and his chin had dropped upon his breast.

"Quick!" the Physician whispered. "Help me turn the bed around."

Quickly the servants rotated the bed like the hands of a clock. But Death's chair stayed still, so that he was now sitting at the foot of the bed of the princess.

Quickly the Physician gave the girl a sip of his golden ale.

And so she sat up and asked for some soup.

Well, the King burst into tears and howled for happiness, while the Queen gathered her daughter to her breast, and all the people applauded, and Death woke up.

He pulled out his pocket watch, and the watch began to chime.

The Physician heard the little chimes. He looked at Death and saw that Death was looking straight back at him.

"Wait," the journeyman brewer cried.

But Death said, "A corpse is wanted. A corpse there shall be." For he played no favorites. None.

Ring, sang the little chime, counting one through four.

Rang, sang the little chime, counting five through eight.

And *Rung*, sang the little chime, counting nine through twelve. *Good night, good night.*

Ring the vesper bell.
I've nothing more to tell.

hegemonica: *n.* form of government distinguished by the supreme dominance of Buddy Greene and his minions

The Older Brother: A Villanelle

by Jonathan Rogers

My brother dragged himself home in disgrace
With ragged clothes and whiskers on his chin.
If I were him, I couldn't show my face.

My brother's life had always been a waste.
We got along quite well without him. Then
My brother dragged himself home in disgrace.

Father cried. The two of them embraced.
The old man let himself be duped again.
If I were him, I couldn't show my face.

The blubbering, the pawing—such poor taste.
All self-respect went out the window when
My brother dragged himself home in disgrace.

How can I love a brother so debased?
Respect a father so benumbed to sin?
If I were him, I couldn't show my face.

Am I the only person in this place
Who still remains the man I've always been?
My brother dragged himself home in disgrace.
If I were him, I couldn't show my face.

On Marriage

by Rebecca Reynolds

We have worked this same farm together
nearly twenty years now.

They didn't tell us when were children changing vows,
wide open as unbroken fields,
that those first thousand mornings
would grow together into one thing—
would become the rest of things.

We turned dry vines over into sod
not knowing we were making soil
for another year's spring.

From the kitchen window
I watched you working that old hoe
into the ungrace of the drought-year.

I saw the strong turn of your back in the sun,
and how your shirt held to your skin.

I traced your lines from a distance,
remembering the slow pulse of your chest,
how it rises and falls in sleep,
and the holy scent of our love.
You worked for me,
and I idolized you,
or hated you.

I needed you
when I should have simply
kneaded the bread.

For you are flesh of my flesh,
bone of my bone,
and there were gifts I could have given.

I could have cradled you
as I have cradled the infants of your seed.

There is rain in the wind today.
There is rain in the wind,
and the loving-kindness of God falls
upon the just
and the unjust alike.
Tomorrow the fields may be soft.

Satilla

by Lanier Ivester

The moment I turned down the rutted lane to Satilla, I knew I shouldn't have come. I had no right; I had forfeited the privilege years ago, and now I felt as though angels barred the way with blazing swords and faces of fire.

I hadn't seen it for the trespass it was until I pulled my little car up beside the rusted Satilla mailbox. The whole idea had seemed such a feasible thing the morning before, sipping coffee in my cool office back in Atlanta, flipping through the stack of foreclosures that had accumulated during my trip to France. Dozens of them: seaside developments that had run out of money, mortgaged-to-the-hilt mansions, family beach cottages on land too tax-burdened too sustain. I turned over one property detail after another with half an eye on my desk clock. Would I have time for a workout and a shower before my lunch with Jim? Then I stopped and stared at the document in front of me as if I had seen a ghost. I had, in fact: at the top of the page was a name I recognized—a name that sent an unexpected arrow through my generally unruffled heart—and I lingered over that sheet of paper until my assistant came in with the mail and an inquisitive cock of her head.

"Everything okay, Ms. Fairchild?" she had asked.

"Yes—yes, Ann," I said "Just going through these foreclosures. What can you tell me about this one?"

I handed the paper across the desk. Ann looked at it, twisting her mouth thoughtfully.

"Hmm, this one's been bank-owned for a decade if I remember. I imagine the house is a dump, but it would have to go anyway. There's a lot of water frontage and room for a deep-water dock. We could get it for a song—you know Parrish County's the next big thing. Property's still dirt cheap down there."

"There aren't any heirs?"

Ann shook her head.

"There was a grandson, I think—he was listed on the foreclosure. But he's out of the country. Brazil if I remember right. No one's been able to get in touch with him."

I sat back in my chair and folded my arms.

"You know, Ann, I think I might run down there myself and have a look at it. Seems a little too good to be true."

Ann grinned conspiratorially. "And the weather's this side of paradise *and* you've got a new convertible," she said with a laugh.

I laughed with her, and if it was a little forced I don't think she noticed.

"Truth is, Provence has ruined me," I told her. "Nothing like a month in the French countryside to make a day in the office intolerable."

And so I went. In an uncharacteristic burst of impulse, I cancelled my lunch with Jim, booked a room in Savannah, and tossed an overnight bag in the trunk of my little roadster. The drive down was a race against the clouds and a revel with the wind. The sunshine, falling full on my uncovered head, was even kinder than it had been in Provence, waking the blood in my veins like the rising sap of an early spring. I took the old roads that wove through pecan orchards and alongside tobacco fields luxuriant in the spring sunshine, and I felt as though I were traveling back into the past with every mile. I was, of course—I had not seen any of these places in twelve years, and I was almost happy as I sped along under that baptism of warm light with my hair snapping against my face in electrifying nips and stings.

But as soon as I reached Satilla, my complacent mood evaporated. What had possessed me to think it wise—to imagine there was any going back? Satilla had landed on my desk amid a stack of foreclosures—one among hundreds of such ruins that Ann turned up every year—but this one was different. This desolation was of a keener sort, deeper and more visceral.

For twelve years I had carried a picture of Satilla in my heart like a miniature painted on ivory, delicate down to the least detail of each green, peaked gable and each grey ringlet of moss curling from the live oaks. I had not taken a single photograph with me when I left on that August night so long ago, supposing never to return, but I did not need any picture to remind me how that drive dipped and twisted under the pines, or how the brown carpet of fallen needles leant a pungent spice to the air. Though it was only April, already the margins were lined with blush-colored primroses, nodding diminutive heads under the shadows of rank grasses, and the salt cedar that feathered the edge of the pinewood was starred with tiny pink blooms.

All these years I had been content to believe that nothing changed in this quiet coastal backwater. I believed that the movement of life in the outside world could not have the least bearing upon the passage of slow days and long, bat-haunted nights. It's a game we adults like to play, I imagine: this mania to pretend that scenes sacred since childhood will remain exactly as we left them, poised in time, the very second hands of the clocks suspended and the breeze holding its breath among the branches of old trees, awaiting only our appearance to resume the business of being and moving and growing older. But to go back is treason—it is a defiance of time's rule and the ruin of our beloved inner vistas. The garden wall that was made of emeralds and gossamer, high as heaven itself, is an ordinary fence after all, fashioned from unremarkable brick and mortar; the roses that were innocence incarnate and gemmed with pearls of dew more precious than diamonds are shaggy and disreputable in their old age, leaning their blowsy heads against one another like crones reminiscent of better days. Once the trespass has been committed—the deed accomplished and the remembered replaced with the real—there is no undoing it.

Despite all forebodings, however, I pressed onward along the drive as if lured by a spell. The little clearing where Uncle Asa's house once stood appeared on the left, only the crumbling stone chimney and the respectful drawing back of the trees attesting to its having been there at all. And then, at the first bend, the old chinaberry where the mockingbirds congregated all winter long, gorging on fruit until, as Uncle Willie J. would have said, they'd made themselves drunk. I slowed my little roadster to a crawl, remembering—so many things: The delicate shadow of a doe moving among palmetto fronds; the song of a killdeer proclaiming its own name; the way we'd strain to catch the first transient hint of salt marsh on the breeze, noses lifted like young spaniels; and how that drive felt on a warm summer night, looking up at the stars as we bounced and rattled our way home in the back of Uncle Willie J.'s truck. I remembered the house lights winking out of the gloom under the oaks and how Aunt Babe's peacocks would split the air with a chorus of murderous screams when Uncle Willie J. announced our arrival by a tap of the tinny old horn. Those peacocks made my blood run cold when they sent up such a ruckus—so like humans calling for help—but Patrick loved them. He used to say they sounded like all the joy and wildness of the world put together.

My heart contracted at the thought of Patrick, with his woodsman's heart and his hopeless impracticality. He was not made for this enlightened world and its movement and speed and its torrential flood of information. He belonged to Uncle Willie J.'s generation—or perhaps to generations even earlier. Patrick's idea of progress was a patch of wooded bottoms cleared of undergrowth for no other reason than that it was pretty to look at, or a recently discovered variety of heirloom tomato plant that—land sakes!—was resistant to both drought *and* humidity. Poor Patrick; he would have been content to live out all his days at Satilla in complete denial that the sprint of civilization had left him behind; unlike me, always raring to go and see and do from the time I was born, desperate to keep up, to surpass, and prove something to the world.

And which of us was the wiser? I wondered, peering up through the canopy of oaks and pines overhead. I stopped my car beneath a moss-hung branch and closed my eyes, thinking of the ruin that surely lay ahead, the dejection of once-tidy barns and the front porch screens sagging in tatters. Aunt Babe's flower beds would be weed-ravaged and Patrick's carefully tended vegetable plot a waste of brome and sandburs. Suddenly I didn't want to go on—I did not want to see Satilla in its demise. I wanted to turn my car around and speed back to Atlanta like I had never known such a place existed or had such ties to it. After all these years the bonds of memory still chafed me raw, though I had never quite known it before. Old associations hovered dangerously near, and like some benighted soul in a fairy tale, I began to feel that if I proceeded much further I would be lost to dark enchantment, unable to return to the world of Atlanta real estate management.

Suddenly a shadow darkened the tree-hung gloom above me and I jumped at the sharp, Amazonian chatter that seemed to explode out of the woods on all sides at once. My fingers tightened on the wheel and then relaxed again as I recognized the massive span and absurdly cocked red head of a pileated woodpecker. "God-A'mighty birds," Uncle Willie J. used to call them, "startlin' a man witless." The shock jarred me out of my reverie. Surely twelve years was safeguard enough between me and all that I wanted to forget; I had taken such pains to ensure it would be. If only regrets weren't so tangled with things I wanted to remember.

I let out the clutch and continued on, faster this time. The only danger was in my head, and I knew it. Uncle Willie J. and Aunt Babe passed on years ago—they were in their upper eighties when I left. And Patrick—well, I'd never have come if Patrick were going to be there.

Soon the white palings of the fence came into view, and then, before I was quite prepared for it, a quick flash of blue as the estuary unfolded under the vaulted aisles of live oaks extending over the lawn like the gnarled and twisted columns of a giant cathedral. I noticed as I drew into the yard that the outbuildings had all been freshly whitewashed, and recently too. The dairy barn before me, the open-sided laundry, the cool little ice house off to the left under a clump of cedars—they all looked as if they had been maintained with immaculate care. This was all a far cry from the desolation I had envisioned. I felt for a moment I must be dreaming. Perhaps I had fallen under an enchantment after all and the past had opened its arms to receive me, prodigal that I was. I stiffened; I wasn't sure I wanted to be received. I had gone away of my own accord and I had come back of my own accord—at least it had seemed so when I made my mind up to undertake this trip. But something not quite canny had been at work from the moment I turned into the drive. I paused getting out of the car, as if fearful of stepping into some kind of ill-fated destiny. It was ridiculous, of course, but the place had that effect on one. As a child, I always felt that Satilla had been waiting for me, whether I was returning from errands in town with Aunt Babe or coming home after a day on the river with Uncle Willie J., and it was the loveliest feeling in the world. But now, as an adult, I wasn't sure I liked it.

I made my way across the gravel-strewn grass to the picket gate leading into the yard. I had been so certain I would find the place unoccupied. But it seemed someone had bought it from the bank and the agent neglected to remove the listing—it happened all the time. At any rate, it was deserted now. There were no cars in the yard where Uncle Willie J.'s old Ford pickup used to reside beside Patrick's battered MG and not a sound issued from either house or barns. I decided to take a look around. Surely no one would object to my holding a little tryst with personal history.

When I ventured into the side yard I saw that Patrick's old vegetable plot had been reclaimed and lately sown. There were neat rows of pepper plants and tomato seedlings in wire cages, and along the farther edge, a company of bamboo teepees supported the mounting tendrils of pole beans. I smiled with unwonted tenderness: Patrick would have been glad to know that someone loved his bit of earth, no matter where on earth he was.

News of Patrick's decampment to Brazil had been unexpected, but it wasn't a complete surprise. What else could he do? I imagined his mortal struggle to save the place, the tooth and nail battle for property taxes and mortgage payments, the scrimping and saving and denial of personal wants and luxuries. And then the sad, slow selling off of the livestock, the empty dairy barn—

I could hardly bear it. I had never in all those years let myself think about what it must have been like for him, but at this first chink in the wall of my reserve I felt a dangerous rush of feeling burgeoning on the other side. Patrick had loved this old place as his own soul; even now, it still bore the mark of his influence in every particular, from the polished brass of the weathervane atop the hay barn to the sun-bleached whelks edging the walks and shrubbery borders. I was almost sorry for whoever had bought Satilla from the bank; they must have felt it was no more theirs than if Patrick Fairchild were still in residence. A prickly feeling shivered up the back of my neck at the thought: was it possible for the living to haunt a place? Or maybe it wasn't the living at all; maybe something had happened to him down in the jungles of Brazil along that black, snake-like river.

A high-pitched, undulating scream split the air at that moment, plaintive as a lost soul, but it did not frighten me. Indeed, it was so much a part of the place that I realized I had been listening for it subconsciously, as if the enchantment were somehow incomplete without it. A moment later the peacock sashayed around the side of the ice house: long, blue neck stretched inquisitively, gaudy crest quivering above the white-fringed eyes. He sized me up for a moment, and then, with a hollow screech, he arched his sinuous neck and shuffled backward and forward a few times, pulsing his tail with the sound of a thousand wings before throwing it up over his head in a green and copper and golden splendor. The notched pupils of a hundred eyes confronted me, and he was so magnificent I wanted to applaud the sight. Then the bird turned his back and flaunted the grey ruffled bloomers of his posterior feathers, dancing and strutting to the blank face of the ice house wall.

"Oh, yes, I remember," I said aloud. "You think you're as pretty from the back as you are from the front."

But I was unnerved, as much at the sound of my own voice in the brooding silence of the place as by the sight of that bird, such a part of my past that he seemed to taunt me with an image of unrecoverable innocence. Did the new owners have a penchant for these royal birds? Did they know that they once thrived here as an honored race? It was entirely plausible that this strutting dandy was a remnant of Aunt Babe's pampered brood; peacocks could live forty years and more if the conditions suited them. Still, the creature's appearance was eerie enough to make me uncomfortable.

The white clapboard house was as unchanged as all the rest, green-shuttered and gracious beneath its bowering trees. Only the flowerbeds skirting the foundation were not as mature as those of Aunt Babe's reign; like the vegetable plot, they looked newly planted, with snapdragons and salvia and old-fashioned dusty miller. But the jasmine shading the front porch was a profusion of glossy leaves and milk-white bloom, spilling a sweetness that nearly broke my heart. When was the last time I had smelled jasmine—*real* jasmine, not the expensive imitation purchased from Saks in a fluted bottled of colored glass? I realized at one whiff of the original that I had been after something in my careful selection of a "signature scent," pursuing a token of things lost forever, a *memento mori* plucked from the ruin of Eden.

I turned away and stumbled over the lawn, sudden tears blinding my eyes. I could hardly bear the reproach of that fragrance and the spectres it summoned more potently than any sight or sound. I hardly knew where I was going, but I was keenly aware of the unforgotten buoyancy of the grass beneath my feet and the fine, black soil sifting in through the straps of my sandals. As I passed under the trees, ghostly moss floated from the branches; the screams of the peacock pursued me like phantoms of my own remorse. Ahead, the river glinted sapphire and diamond, pulsing against the green fringe of marsh in an endless caress. And through that burning haze of unshed tears I picked out the form of a curving bench, wrapped at the base of one of the live oaks near the shore. It was still there.

Uncle Willie J. had made it for me when I was a little girl lately come to live with them at the old family home. No one else had even the imagination, much less the kindness, to call me family; it was a stretch even I was unwilling to claim. But the people of Satilla had felt otherwise, though heaven knew why. For as long as I could remember I had known what it meant to be unwanted; even as a tiny child my own mother had made me keenly aware of my superfluity, well before the night she left me in the care of an indifferent sitter and flounced off on a date with no intention of ever coming back. The shadowy, half-remembered adults upon whose care I was cast pretended to be shocked—and pretended that I was too young to understand what had happened. No one is too young to fathom abandonment, though; it's an invisible brand that marks you for life, and no amount of innocence can diminish that angry scar. Even in foster care I felt the scorch of it; no one seemed to know quite what to do with such a willful, fearful urchin as I had become, and by the time I was eight years old I had lived in five different houses in five different families. Not one of them was home.

But with these Fairchilds, it was different. When they tracked me down—my mother was a distant cousin on Aunt Babe's side—I was already wild as a colt and twice as intractable. And yet, they had seen something in that unlovable scrap of humanity and loved it—in spite of itself. They had taken me home to Satilla on a hazy afternoon in late summer, and there I remained till I was twenty-two and mad with ambition, aching to get away and make my mark on the world.

In spite of all my fiery independence, however, I had kept one tie to the old life and these people who had been so good to me—to their own hurt. I took the name Fairchild for my own, assuming it both professionally and personally, though I had never done anything about it from a legal standpoint. I always loved that name and yearned to claim it—and for it to claim me. It sounded so lovely in my ears, like an endearment.

Fairchild. All I had ever wanted to be—and all I would never be, though every court in the land proclaimed it so. A real Fairchild would never behave the way I had.

I smiled sadly. Uncle Willie J. had carved my name there in the rough bark of the tree, telling me it meant I belonged to Satilla and to them, no matter what others might say. It had to be well grown over by now, it was so long ago and beginning to fade even before I left. But I remembered him there in the sunshine of a hot summer day, chiseling away with his horn-handled pocketknife, so intent on his work he scarcely seemed to notice the gnats that buzzed and retreated incessantly around his eyes and nose and mouth. And when he was done, he grinned in a way that made me suddenly want to cry, it was so kind, and his faded blue eyes shone behind the thin-rimmed spectacles he always wore. He had added a heart with an arrow through it beneath my name—it seemed almost prophetic to think of it now.

My eyes sought the spot instinctively, just to the left of a notched artery running along the length of the trunk. "That's where the tree's heart is," Uncle Willie J. had said. I expected to find a smooth patch reclaimed by bark and years of growth, but instead there was a lightness of exposed wood, a bit of tree-flesh gleaming gold from out of the dark expanse.

Sally. My own name, and lately carved. I was bewildered: just like everything else I had encountered on this dreamlike day, here was reclamation where I had expected ruin, right down to the little arrow-pierced heart.

I sat down and stared at the little engraving until my eyes hurt, and the sealed-off places in my heart began to tremble. Hot waves of shame began to gather and heave within me, dredging up unredeemable things, and with a loathing I never thought myself capable of, I contemplated the vilest creature I have ever known: *myself.* For twelve years and more I had refused to look at the image in that fateful glass of self revelation, turning my face toward ambition and accomplishment, relationships, business deals, European vacations—anywhere but toward the truth.

And the truth was simple, if appalling: I had made my way in the world with great success, made a name that was beginning to be known in my field and beyond—but I had done it to the utter ruin of the people who had given me that name.

When Uncle Willie J. heard of the restaurant scheme in Savannah, he had been dubious, but he heard me out with that kingly humility of his and asked insightful questions that I managed to dither my way around. All I needed was the money—I already had the connections, a chef lined up, an unshakable marketing plan. People in Savannah—people whose opinions I cared about—were beginning to talk of my enterprise and ingenuity, "so unusual in a woman her age," and on more than one occasion since graduating from college I had been called "that young entrepreneur from Satilla." I was intoxicated by what was being said of me, by what was being said that I could do—even more so, by what I *knew* I was going to do.

"I'll make you rich, Uncle Willie J.," I had said, with unforgivable conceit. And he had laughed in that low, soft way of his and shaken his head.

"I don't want to be rich, sugar," he said. "I got everything I want, right here. But I do want you to be happy."

And so, he had given me the money, money that had been saved for Patrick's college education from the day he was born. And when that was not enough, he had mortgaged Satilla in order to give me more.

The restaurant failed. Of course it did. I could acknowledge that plainly now, though it was a fiery brand to my soul at the time. The business was too competitive, the competitors too established, the location itself a block too far off center. But even in failure it had given me a boost and thrown me in the path of those who could appreciate my talents. An opportunity with a big development firm opened in New York and I seized it without a backward glance. I always meant to return—I was too proud to be ashamed of my failure, and I was determined that when I did come back it would be with laurels on my brow and a check in my hand to cover the mortgage. One thing led to another, however; life made demands that my impossible schedule and early salary had been scarcely able to answer. The years slipped away like beads off a broken strand.

It was reprehensible, of course, what I'd done—indefensible and heartbreakingly final. But for my pride, Uncle Willie J. and Aunt Babe would have lived out their lives beneath these paternal trees, resting at last from their long labor in one of those high-ceilinged rooms under a lacy canopy made by Aunt Babe's great-great Someone-or-Other. Patrick would have gone to college, and the farm would have been here waiting for him when he came back. And Satilla would be alive. Alive as—as it seemed to be this very moment. Only there were no Fairchilds to make it the very outskirts of heaven with their courtly kindness and old-fashioned ways.

I fingered the carved legend in the tree and my heart surged with grief. If only there were something I could do—some amends I could make. I turned and looked out over the water, blinding now in the late afternoon glare. The form of a shrimp boat was just coming into view, riggings uplifted like enormous wings. A wheeling company of gulls escorted it across the estuary and their lithe forms were black at this distance and agile as a troupe of dancers. Tears ran down my face and dropped onto my hands folded helplessly in my lap.

I watched the boat until it was out of sight, rounding the bend at Mudcat Landing. Then I got up with a sigh, smoothed my skirt, and turned to look back at the house. I had been here long enough—had seen enough and been reminded of enough. I both longed and hated to leave.

As I was passing back under the trees, I heard the rumble of a motor coming along the drive, and a moment later, an old Ford pickup, nearly as ramshackle as Uncle Willie J.'s had been, drew up alongside my little convertible. The door opened and a ragbag of a dog exploded out of the cab, dancing in impatient circles until a tennis ball was likewise ejected and pitched over the hedges towards the lawn on which I stood. The dog hurtled after the ball, ears, tail and tongue all flying, until, seeing me, he rerouted his joyful gallop in my direction. I stooped to meet him, but immediately stood up again with a shriek. He reeked of river water and saw fit to nudge his sandy head against my sundress before passing proper introductions.

I petted him gingerly until his owner appeared, half-whistling, half-laughing, striding towards us over the grass. I watched him come with a cold, creeping sense of unreality and a heart that felt like it had turned to ice. Here was one more shock, and this one so outrageous it made my head spin. The man was Patrick Fairchild.

"Hey there, Sal," he said in that lazy drawl of his, just exactly as if we had parted only that morning and not twelve years ago.

I found my voice with some effort.

"Patrick? What—what are you doing here?"

He grinned, and the eyes that twinkled out of his tanned face were blue as swamp irises.

"Livin' here."

"But I—I thought—" I floundered helplessly and then plunged in again, all civilities aside. "I thought you lost the farm. I thought you were in Brazil."

Patrick nodded, still grinning in a way that made me so self conscious I felt my soul had been turned inside out. How could he look at me with such warmth? I wanted to turn my face away.

"I did lose the farm—we did, I mean. Grandmother and Grandaddy were still alive then."

"Oh, God," I groaned. "Tell me they didn't have to endure all that."

"They died happy, Sal," Patrick said, suddenly grave. "I saw to that—before I went to Brazil. Grandmother had a cousin over towards Long Marsh that could take them in, and I took a room nearby. Grandaddy didn't live a year after that, and Grandmother followed him by six months. But I tell you, Sal, they were happy. They always were, you know."

I knew it, though I couldn't have spoken at that moment if I were threatened at knifepoint.

"After they were gone there wasn't much for me here, so I joined a team that was working with farmers along the Amazon—bringing newfangled methods to the natives and all that, and they needed some farmers to show them how things were done. Well, the upshot is that the good people of Brazil taught me a thing or two about growing rice, and the minute I could scrape together enough pennies to convince the bank to give me a loan, I came back. Found the old place was still for sale. Too rambling and old-fashioned for modern tastes, I suppose. But I can't help thinking some good energy was at work in keeping it on the market. You know it started as a rice plantation, back in the day."

"How long have you been back?"

"'Bout six months," he replied, stroking his grizzled chin. "Took me nearly ten years to save the money."

He named the awful thing with such grace and another of those lopsided smiles. "Patrick, I—I'm so sorry," I said lamely.

"Tried to put everything back the way it was," he went on, as if he had not heard me, "you know, the way things were when we were kids. Even got a peacock—traded four hens for him off old Jefferson down at New Stirling."

I swallowed a scorching lump in my throat. "Patrick, there has to be something I can do—some way I can help—"

"See your name?" he said with boyish shyness, jerking his head towards the great tree at the water's edge.

I nodded.

"Just got around to that last week. Grandaddy's carving was mostly gone. I hope it's a good enough replica."

"It's perfect," I said.

He smiled and stretched out his hand. It was even more brown and calloused than I remembered and the nails were stained with the sandy black loam of the rice fields.

"C'mon, Sal. You're just in time for supper," he said. "It was a good day on the river and I've got such a mess of white perch it'll make you cry. I bet you haven't had anything that sweet since you left."

I looked down at his hand and hesitated. I felt like it would burn me if I touched it.

"Patrick, you—you don't seem to understand."

"Understand what?" he asked, patting his leg with a low whistle to the dog.

"I have to make amends."

He looked at me keenly, sifting my heart with those blue eyes of his.

"Amends?" he echoed quizzically. "You're talkin' out of your head, Sal. You think any amount of amends'll bring back the dead—dead times or dead folks?" His smile was gentler than ever as he reached for my hand once more and gripped it in a firm clasp. "I ain't got sisters to spare, Sal. No sense splittin' hairs over things that can't be undone. You're here and want to be—that's amends enough."

I walked with him back to the house and watched as he pulled Uncle Willie J.'s archaic fish fryer out of the shed and filled it with Wesson oil. While he cleaned and cooked the fish he told me about his hopes for the first crop of rice, how if all went well he'd have enough to make the payments to the bank and live on here in spartan simplicity.

"I'm happy, Sal," he said. "Happier than ever now you're here. You've always got a home to come to, and Fairchilds got to stick together in this old world."

I'm not a Fairchild, the words leapt to my lips. But I did not utter them. Instead, I took the rickety wooden folding chair that he held out for me before a table spread with an old checkered cloth and a series of mismatched Willow ware. I watched as he lowered a couple of perch onto my plate, battered and crisped to golden perfection. The dog of unidentifiable breed lowered his head on my lap and swished his great tail against my ankles, lifting prayerful eyes towards my plate. I took a hushpuppy from the basket Patrick offered, burning my fingers in the process, and bowed my head as he mumbled a modest grace for the food. Then I smiled at him across the table, and in a wash of evening light that turned everything in its path to gold, I took a bite.

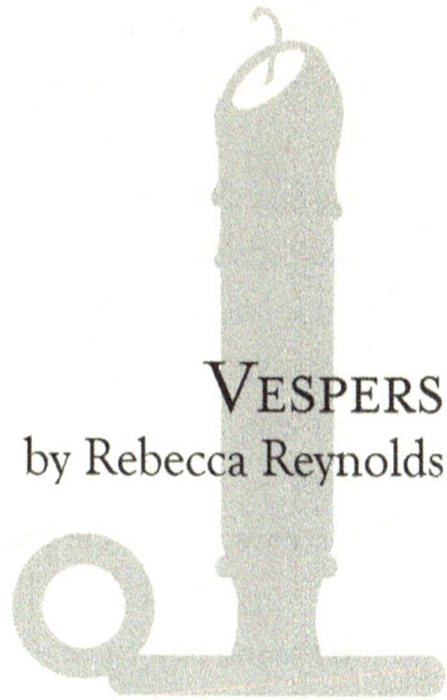

Vespers

by Rebecca Reynolds

She was the sort of woman
who committed sins forgiven only of men.

It was not to be helped.

The book of Proverbs made her restless.
The book of Psalms made her weep.
She learned what was hot
by sticking her hands in the fire.
Poison she knew by ingestion.

She learned that love inflames,
that hate infects,
and that honesty can be brave,
or damned foolish
—or both.

She arrived also at anger,
for it seemed

that from her first day
God had set His traps at her feet.

She had thrown her arms into goodness
elbow-deep
and found it lacking,
excessive,
desperate,
silent.
There were rules she could never keep.

So she stared into heaven like an arrow
drawn for release
and strode the earth
upon rotting floors
primed to fall through
into hell.

Each night she slept with her window open
not repeating her vespers.

One strong leg she bent outside the blanket
as if it were running.
Breath billowed inside her chest.
Her lifeblood pulsed, slowly,
and the October wind
caught up the curtains, danced,
and tossed grace freely,
like a child throwing handfuls of violets.

Notes from the Sea

by Rebecca Reynolds

Stepping two bare feet in salted, sighing recessions,
I crossed a chorus,
grace, upon grace,
upon grace.

The seaside runs white-laced and popping,
sizzles, tickles my ankles, sucks at my toes,
impresses the full-roaring strength of mighty miles of ocean,
soft as a husband, upon my land-sore bones.

Waves tease the earth from beneath my feet
until I laugh,
unsteadied,
arms cast out like a child catching her balance.

I am vain enough to measure my own feet
against the prints others have left.
I am ugly and too big,
though I leave no mark at all upon the sand.
I have learned to place my weight lightly, at the least.

In the secrecy of evening,
I press my sole into forms left by the beautiful ones,
like a servant trying on crowns.

I feel the cool, deep heel-caves left by the confident,
and I wonder what it is like
to run the earth with such surety.

Here is a neat, even row of toes.
They dig each step into earth
as if they might cling to it.

And see there! Such pretty, high arches.
A dancer, perhaps?
Someone holds those feet in his lap at night.
He touches them and is proud of them.
He marvels at their delicacy.

It takes courage to measure my foot
against the expanse left by a work boot.
Mine is smaller by two inches.
Thank God,
I am less than I have feared.

"Love, upon love,
such vast deep love."
The seaside sighs,
as if it meant love for me;
and so I walk lightly,
leaving no trace,
afraid of breaking his pursuit.

Pelicans, seven in a line,
Fly, bellies nearly touching the water,
Rise, like notes on a stave.

Black-legged birds with yellow socks
run silly from waves,
making of themselves a spectacle.

A lost feather rolls in the sigh's recession,
a third of a cigarette,
broken brown shells,
and blue ones turning,
one perfect white half-shell,
serene,
rim-down, waiting.

Upon the rain-pocked sand,
each wave stretches, yawns,
makes a mirror darkly,
casts the sky back to the heavens.

soggage: *n.* a thoroughly wetted suitcase.

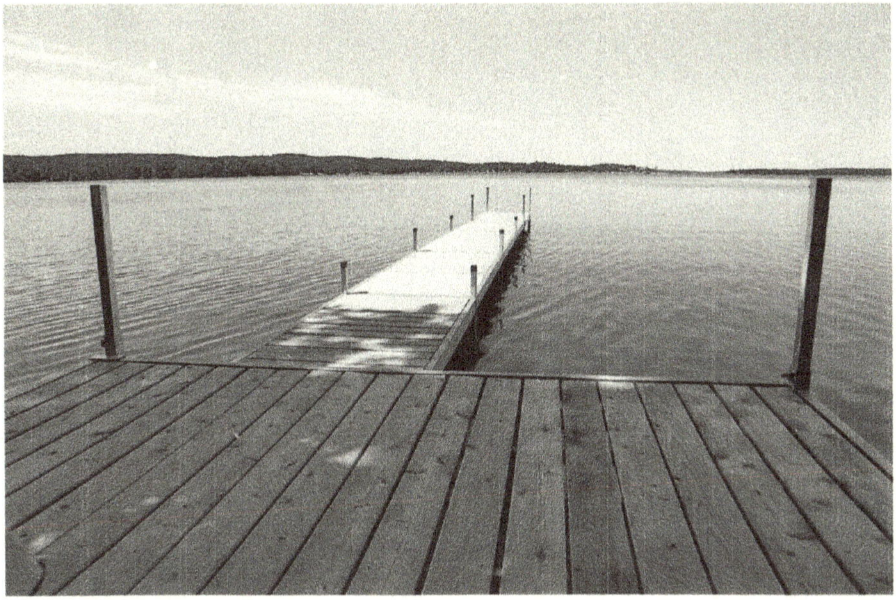

The Far Side of the Sea

by Eric Peters

Like the dot of an overturned question mark, I crouched on the dock. My heart weighing anchor, setting out to answer the dawn, I sought the far side of the sea, but my vessel foundered on the shoals. Struggling ashore, fearful of every shadow, howling a fearsome anger, mired in exhaustion, my heart turned bitter, withered, and grew old, leaving me marooned and alone, a period on an empty page. Though I died a death there, the mystery wasn't the dying. The mystery was the rescue and the living that followed, the new sentence taking form.

obloot: *n.* stolen treasure that is somewhat longer than it is wide

The Younger Brother: A Villanelle

by Jonathan Rogers

I don't know how I'm going to show my face.
I never thought I'd see this town again.
But here I stand: I've come home to disgrace.

Shall I shuffle in? With downcast eyes abase
Myself before him? Or pull that old, sly grin?
I don't know how I'm going to show my face.

I've got a plan. I know I can't erase
The shame, but I can join his hired men—
Say, "Here I stand. I've come home to disgrace."

I'll show him that I've changed. I know my place.
I've forfeited his love from way back then.
I don't know how I'm going to show my face.

But now he races toward me to embrace
The son he loves. He doesn't listen when
I stutter, "Here I stand. I've come home to disgrace."

His love besieged my shame and laid it waste.
And do you think I'll be the same again?
I don't. No, now I'm going to show my face.
Here I stand. I've come home to this grace.

The Summer of the Mustard Tree

by Sarah Clarkson

"I want to buy a mustard seed. Please."

Lila plunked her hands down on the garden store counter. She was seven years old, but she had the gumption of David when he stared down Goliath. When she took hold of an idea, her face turned pixie sharp and her lips pursed themselves into a tight red knot and neither angel nor demon could stand in her way until the thing was achieved.

"Is ten dollars enough?"

"Ten dollars? Lord have mercy, child! You planning to start a mustard farm?" Joe stared down at his tiny, golden-haired customer. His dark brown eyes betrayed a sweet spirit. He leaned toward Lila and hitched up one eyebrow. "Ten cents is more like it. What do you need mustard for anyway? You like the greens?"

"No, sir." Lila wrinkled her freckled nose at the thought of mustard greens. "My momma likes them, but I hate 'em," she said, shaking her head in disgust. "I want to grow a mustard tree."

Joe's long fingers tapped the counter. "A tree, huh? I don't think mustard seeds usually—"

"Like the one in the Bible."

"Oh. Right." Joe's fingers tap-danced on the countertop. "Wait," he said, and his fingers stopped. "Your big brother is Cal Armstrong, right?"

"Yessir," Lila said with some suspicion.

"Hear he's been right sick lately. That true?"

"Yessir. My brother's been real sick, and I aim to help him get better. Bible says a mustard tree is a miracle."

"Uh huh. So, you plan to grow this, uh, mustard tree in your mama's garden, is that it? I helped her plan that garden, but I don't recall any talk of mustard."

"It's not her plan. It's mine," Lila replied. "I got a place at the back, by the fence, near the gate."

The sudden thud of Joe's hands on the countertop jerked Lila's head up. Joe turned abruptly and headed toward an old oak cabinet that hulked ten feet away in one of the aged store's shadowy corners. It was tall as Joe, wide as a doorway, knobbed and smudged with age and use, and crossed from top to bottom with lines of small, square drawers with black handles, each with a tiny faded label. Joe jerked one drawer open and took something from it.

"Mustard seeds," Joe said, smacking a small white packet on the counter in front of Lila. "There you are, little miss. Just what the customer ordered."

Lila picked up the package as though it was fragile, running her finger over the seven black letters that spelled out exactly what she wanted them to. Carefully, she stowed the seed packet in her satchel and made sure it was secure. Then she pulled a wrinkled ten-dollar bill from her pocket, and held it out to Joe.

"Nope. This mustard's on the house," said Joe. "You just let me come see it when it grows, okay?" Joe raised an eyebrow and grinned.

So rare was his smile, so unexpected the gentle gleam of his face when it came, that Lila was undone. She laughed out loud. "Okay. See ya, Joe."

Out the door she ran, elation in every step. She was small for her age but sturdy and brown from the sun. She wore overalls every day that she could, and kept bare feet as often as her mother would let her. As she skipped homeward, her whole body expressed a childlike vim. The late afternoon sun slanted down, low and honeyed through the leaves of old maples and oaks guarding the streets of her tiny southern town. The heat of early summer had settled into the pavement and now it steeped in the air. As it warmed Lila's face, all she could think was, *perfect planting weather*. She ran faster. If she was quick, she could plant her seed before supper.

Joe stepped into the doorway of the garden store to watch her scurry away. A quiet settled over his face like the swift fall of dusk. He folded his arms across his overalls, and as Lila skipped up the street, all the sunlight of his smile faded. When she turned the corner and ran out of sight, he flipped the "Open" sign in his window to "Closed" and pulled the shop door shut.

He made his way back to the counter and leaned over it, planting his elbows full on its top, his chin propped in his hands. Dusk flowed in, chasing the daylight out of the glass jars of candy. Shadows slowly crept over the slat-board boxes of seeds and bulbs and blanketed the shelves of garden tools that crowded his shop. The shadows finally embraced Joe too, but still, he did not move. Night came full.

Then—*smack*—up went his elbows and down came his hands on the counter. He turned to face the huge oak cabinet. The jerk of a string gave him light from a bare bulb overhead and he stooped down to the farthest, darkest corner drawer. He pulled it all the way out and removed a single item.

In the palm of one of his large, work-creased hands sat a little wooden box—dark hardwood with dovetailed corners and star-like designs inlaid upon its lid. It seemed like a box to hold a ring, a gem, or something precious. But this was a seed store. He set it on the counter, and stared down at it. Light glimmered afresh in his eyes. His fingers drummed a dance on the glass. He smiled.

A plump moon hung in the sky, spilling silver over the early evening landscape. Its light was a guide to Lila's hands as she dug out the soil with her garden spade. She took the seed packet from her satchel, removed an almost imperceptible mustard seed from it, placed it deep in the hole, pulled the dirt over it, and patted the last of the warm soil into place. She added some extra soil from her mother's garden so she could build up a nice mound over her seed. It was like the mountain in the Sunday School lesson. Jesus had said, "faith like a mustard seed" would move mountains, and one dull gem of a mustard seed now lay pillowed in the earth. One only had been prescribed, so one was what she must plant. Miracles required precision. She stowed the rest of the seeds in her satchel, sat back on her heels, and let her eyes adjust to the dim, moon-beamed garden and yard behind her house.

This was her special realm, a private kingdom enclosed by a high, whitewashed fence covered with ivy hanging in a riotous curtain that protected her from the eyes of the curious world. An oak stood in its middle, stately as an ancient king and just as arthritic, limbs skewed in dignified deformity. His queen, an aged apple lady, held court in the farthest corner. Lila climbed up now into the branches of the apple tree and settled into her favorite spot, a curved intersection where she could sit with her back to the trunk. This was the throne from which she inspected her realm and watched the stars.

It was in that place, high amidst the shimmering, whispering leaves, that she spent her summer days. She would go there to read, to think, and to spy on the myriad dramas played out by clouds in the sky. The tree could be her ship for exploring, or a mountain to climb, but mostly it was her castle. Her fortress. Here, nothing frightened her, not even the night with its darkness and danger.

Lila turned her gaze from the stars to look across the yard toward the house. From where she sat, she could see into her second-story bedroom window, with its pink curtains and lace at the sill. Her room was not like her tree. It should be a place of comfort, but it was not. She dreaded the fall of night in that little room.

For the past four nights, Lila had awakened at two in the morning. Each time, she'd known by the quilt-like hush muffling the house that the night was at its deepest. Her eyes had widened in the blackness as she woke with that acute but fogged awareness that visits only those who yearn most for sleep. The memory of sirens had become an alarm clock in her soul. For on her first sleepless night, the sirens had been real and so to had been the eerie red slash of ambulance lights down her clean white walls. Voices had jolted her from deep sleep—her mother's pitched and tight with fear, her brother Cal's far weaker, both overruled by the strident directives of the medics invading her home.

Lila had lain in bed with her pillow over her face until her mother stumbled in and switched on the light. The brazen glare made her squirm farther under her covers, but she wriggled out quickly when her mother said in a soft, foggy voice, "Hurry, hon. Get dressed. Cal's not doing so well and we've got to get him to the hospital."

Since then, the darkened silence of her bedroom had echoed nightly with memories of that first night. Like a shadow, fear had crept into her room. Lila hated to be afraid. But she was about to fix that.

From her perch in the tree, Lila shifted in the moonlit branches and held to one like a monkey. She leaned out until she could see the mound of fresh-turned dirt in the far corner of the garden. One mustard seed, just like the pastor said. *One mustard seed and a great pile of faith to go with it.* Those words had reached her like a revelation, for she hadn't been able to think of what she could do to help Cal, or to heal the fear in her mother's voice. But faith she had. Mustard seeds she could get. And now they both were in place.

"Lila? Lila!"

A woman's voice called impatiently into the darkness and jolted Lila from her thoughts.

"Coming, Mama."

Lila swung down, hung for a moment, then dropped to the ground. She ran toward the house, slowing to grab her garden spade, but at sight of the mound of fresh soil went down on her knees. She planted a kiss where the mustard seed lay buried. The scent of earth came to her, and with it the tang of hidden things waiting to grow. Soon, as water and sunlight gave strength to the little seed, it would make its leap toward the sun. Comfort grew within her, as if her heart were a tiny golden seed that reached for the sunlight too.

"Lila. Dinner. Now!"

Lila scurried through the shadows of the oak tree, covering her head for fear of the fruit bats that might swoop down and bite her ear. As Lila approached the porch and skipped up the steps, her mother swung open the storm door and Lila bounded into the house.

"Hey, Mama."

Helen Armstrong stood on the porch, fists on her hips and brown eyes snapping. Her face was flushed from cooking, her dark hair damp with the humid summer night. Lila smiled up at her mother, but cringed when she caught sight of the crease above her right eyebrow.

"I called three times. Where were you?"

"I was planting something. Sorry, Mama."

Lila's lip curled down and her eyes became very large. The hard line above her mother's eye disappeared at the hint of anxiety in Lila's countenance.

"What were you planting?" Helen put her hand on Lila's shoulder and pulled her toward the glow of the kitchen, shutting the porch door behind them.

"It's a secret," said Lila. Still pink-cheeked from her dash across the yard, she squirmed into her chair at the kitchen table. Helen glanced back at her daughter with a lift of that eyebrow, but turned to the stove as the dull plunk of boiling soup caught her attention. A round loaf of fresh bread cooled in the center of the table and fueled Lila's fierce hunger. She would have pinched off a bite if her mother's eye hadn't shot her way before she could try.

"Where's Cal, Mama?"

"Right here, squirt. Supper ready?"

Cal's husky tones brought the room to a hush. Mother and daughter turned at the same instant, faces abruptly poised, bodies tensed as if to catch something that might break. Cal shuffled to the table, brown hair standing at fantastic angles from his head. At fourteen years, he was taller than his mother, built strong like his father, and had the Armstrong grin always at the ready. Cal's easy grace belied the cancer relentlessly attacking his body. The chemo had left him depleted and drained. Sleepiness flushed him red and he was still in his pajamas. He grinned at Lila and slumped into his chair.

"This is the life," he said. "Sleep all day and wake up to eat."

"How are you feeling, sweetie?" Helen reached out to feel Cal's head as she set a soup bowl on the table in front of him.

"I'm fine."

The answer was too quick, too sure. But he said it with a grin—always that grin.

"You want some milk, Cal?" Lila's voice was eager with anticipation.

"Sure, squirt. A big glass. I'm thirsty."

Lila's chair screeched as she shoved it back and ran to the refrigerator. It was a risky business, getting the gallon-size jug maneuvered into place. She had to set the glass on the floor, but she managed with only a few drops spilled, and presented the glass to her brother with a look of triumph on her face.

"Thanks, you," he said, and patted her head.

While Lila took the milk jug back to the refrigerator and found a rag to clean up her spill, Helen leaned over the table to speak to Cal in a low, hurried voice. When Lila came back, her mother sat up straight, smiled at her daughter, and turned deliberately to her soup. Lila had become accustomed to these surreptitious conversations and knew not to ask any questions.

"Cal, say the blessing," Helen commanded as he picked up his spoon.

"For what we are about to receive, may the Lord make us truly thankful," Cal said, rushing, then set to eating with diligence.

Lila ate slowly, her mind set on her mother and brother and the way they avoided looking too long at one another. Quiet crept in like a cat and curled up at the leg of the table. The steam of fresh bread and hot soup fogged up the kitchen window, sealing the three of them into the sensory warmth of a family kitchen.

As Cal ate and the night sky darkened, Lila watched her mother's body yield to the calm of the moment; the stiff movement of her arms gentled in response to the warmth, the food, and Cal's healthy appetite. Worry and care temporarily left the room. Lila looked through the steamy window to where the stars began to fill the night sky. The blackness beyond the light seemed not empty but friendly, for burrowed in its hush lay the promise of Lila's mustard seed.

It was deep in the night, under the cover of a now moonless sky, when a lean figure opened the back gate and crept into the Armstrong garden. With the dim beam of an old flashlight showing the way, the figure moved slowly through the darkness until it reached the back fence and knelt before Lila's mound of earth. The figure surveyed the fresh planting, and then with a pair of long, lean hands dug into the earth until the hole that Lila had made with her spade was open again. The two-handed scoop of soil with Lila's mustard seed in it went into a burlap bag. The figure then took a small wooden box out of its overall pocket. The careful fingers removed the lid from the box, and dropped something into the hole. The figure knew just where to go to find more soil and soon piled warm earth back into that empty place and patted it down. The figure stood, tall and thin in the shadows, and then was gone. The back gate clicked quietly. A hush, thick as the coming dew, settled back upon the garden.

When the first green tip of a sprout stuck its tiny fist in the air a few days later, Lila was proud as a new mother. For most of that first morning, she lay on her stomach and stared at it, nose to nose with her newborn seedling. Every minute or so, she reached out a finger to tap the slender stem, then glanced up to see if rain might be coming. When her mother, wash pins in her mouth as she hung out the laundry, suggested that infant plants, unlike humans, might not thrive if touched so often, Lila, big-eyed, kept her hands under her chin. But she did not cease to stare.

Only when Cal helped her rig a tiny cage of wire over the frail shoot did she agree to forsake its company and scurry in to lunch. Ten minutes later, she was back. She kept a steady vigil the rest of that afternoon to monitor her precious seedling's growth. When night fell and her mother summoned her inside, she worried that no visible growth had occurred that day. But by dawn, the hearty little plant had grown half an inch, and Lila rejoiced mightily. Soon she curbed her fretting, as it was plain her seedling knew well enough how to grow without her.

When Lila's hints and gulped excitement finally prompted her mother to ask what was so special about the plant, Lila grabbed her hand and bellowed at her brother, "Cal, you can't listen!" Lila pulled her mother into the kitchen and shut the door.

"It's a mustard seed, Mama," she whispered with great importance, hands cupped around her mouth. "And you've got to have faith. Like me." And that was all the explanation Helen was to get, for the next instant her sprite of a child was out the door, leaping toward the corner of the yard where her plant held court.

Rather than entering into Lila's excitement, Helen stood with her hands twisting in and out of each other, as if in search of something she could not find. Her knees felt abruptly weak and she sank into a chair at the kitchen table. It was beyond her how any one mother could figure the right thing to do or how to keep her child's heart from breaking. Sunday School had always seemed a good idea, but what was a mother to do when it kindled such wild, impossible dreams? Pastors were forever urging people to have faith like a child's—blind, impossible faith. But what was a mother to do if her child's faith was dashed?

Lila's golden head shimmered and bobbed in the afternoon sunlight as Helen stared out the window. It was hard enough that the war had taken Lila's father, and worse almost that she had to see her brother battling cancer. But if that golden child lost all her shimmer and life because of a mustard seed, well—Helen sighed. The Almighty had his work cut out for him.

The wonder began on the first of July. Helen was serving old Gladys Hunt a cup of tea in the garden. At a round patio table in the shade of a large umbrella, Lila sipped cambric tea sweetly with her mother and Aunt Gladys, gobbled her cake without smacking once, and dashed off, asking to be excused five steps after leaving.

Her mother smiled and leaned closer to the older woman, now in her late seventies. "I hope you'll excuse Lila. She's gone to inspect her mustard plant." As they looked over their shoulders, Lila made her way to the corner of the garden where her plant now reached out to the sun with several lithe green arms decorated with slim, curled leaves.

"Oh really," Aunt Gladys said, nodding politely. "How nice she's interested in gardening. My mother got me started when I was about her age."

Helen blushed. "Well, actually, I don't think she's that interested in gardening. Lila has got the idea into her head that a mustard seed has some kind of miraculous power. She got the notion from a Sunday School lesson about the parable." Helen shook her head. "I think she believes that if she can grow a mustard tree, it will somehow help Cal." Helen gripped her teacup perilously and turned to her friend with a pleading look of surrender. "I know, I know, Gladys. I ought to tell her it can't help, but that plant makes her so happy and to spoil it for her, well, it's like stomping on a rose, isn't it?"

Gladys smiled, leaned close to Helen and nodded with sympathy. "Of course, dear." She straightened back up and asked, "Do you think she'd let me see her plant? I've always been quite the gardener, you know. The arthritis has slowed me down a little, but I love to bring things to life."

"Slowed you down? You've got the best garden in town and everyone knows it, Gladys. I'm sure Lila would love to show it to you. She's quite proud of it." Helen helped Aunt Gladys off her chair and over to the shade-dappled corner where Lila sat Indian-style next to her plant. Gladys knelt down and reached out a gnarled hand to brush the sturdy young growth. Lila was about to stop her, but held back when she noticed the eyebrow her mother lifted in her direction.

"It's a healthy thing, isn't it?" said the old woman. Her approval brought a blush of pride to Lila's cheeks. "But, dear, I've never seen a mustard plant like this. I've never seen these leaves at all. Are you sure it's mustard, Lila?"

Lila merely pulled her satchel from behind her and produced the crumpled seed packet. "See," she said, pointing. "It says so right on front. *Mustard.*"

"Yes, I see that it does," said Aunt Gladys. "It's a lovely plant. Thank you for letting me see it, dearie." Lila smiled, watched as they left, and then turned back to her plant.

The two women trundled through the garden and back to the table to finish their tea. They sat quietly for a few minutes, and then Gladys turned to Helen. "I've never seen that plant before. I don't think it's a mustard, but I'm baffled. No idea what it actually is. I'm going home to look through my books." With that, the old woman rose and took her leave.

Lila leaned in close to her plant, nose-to-nose with the tip of the first leaf. She studied it carefully and knew every fiber, bend, branch, and leaf on it. It bothered her a little that the plant didn't look like the picture on her seed packet. But the one great fact of the healthy plant itself was the only detail she cared about. She hadn't yet thought to wonder whether her plant could be something other than mustard. She simply believed that it was. And she believed it would help Cal.

The summer went by steadily. The plant grew, and Lila's gladness grew with it. Every day it more and more resembled a tiny tree, its slim young arms woven in a tangle of green branches that twined a higher with each new rising of the sun. Soon, the leaves began to unfold—long, slender fingers veined in silver, with a tiny bud at the base of each one. When a fresh wind leapt through the yard, the whole little tree shimmered and laughed. Perched in her apple tree, or lying on the grass, Lila laughed with it, and hope rushed through her like a fresh, sweet wind.

Cal was growing stronger too. His once-pale face now boasted a healthy and gladsome flush. He woke earlier, moved more confidently, and ate with an appetite worthy of a teenage boy. The pain that had shadowed his demeanor had gone and he was like a new person in the house. He even pestered his mother into allowing him to throw a few easy balls with his friends. When she agreed, he picked her up and swung her around in his arms.

Lila's laughter rang like silver rain through the rooms of the old house and Cal's own thunderous laughter answered. To Helen the whole house seemed freshened, quickened with life, as hope blew in a sweet storm through each room.

After a month of steady growth, the little tree was as tall as Lila, with a dozen healthy branches—and a new wonder about to emerge. Lila discovered it early one morning. Her shriek of delight drew her mother, sleepy and stumbling, robe trailing loose behind her, into the garden. Lila pointed at her discovery: from one of the tiny buds a small crimson flower had bloomed. She and her mother hugged each other excitedly, jumping with simple joy. Helen quietly admired the flower with her young daughter, commenting on its sharp red petals and center of gold. She didn't even flinch when Lila, shouting her intent to wake Cal, and bounded off barefoot to do so.

Soon after, the pilgrimage began. Before the bloom there had been nothing more than small talk about town—a new report here, a chuckle there, a shaken head, a sympathetic smile. But with the new bloom, there was heightened curiosity. People wanted to see the thing now, not just talk about it.

Molly Jones was the first. She was the slim, young mother of Katy, Lila's best friend. Lila was playing at Katy's house that day, so Helen was a bit confused when Molly showed up at the front door.

"Hello, Helen." Molly, proper and prim, stood formally just inside the open door as she spoke. "I know this may seem like an unusual request, but I was wondering if I might take a quick look at Lila's plant."

Helen motioned her in and assured her that it was not at all unusual, and that of course she could see the plant. They walked straight through the house and out to the backyard. Molly bent down to examine the red bloom. She regarded it with something close to reverence. Then she straightened back up to her prim posture, and turned to speak.

"While Lila has been at my house this morning, she's been going on and on about a miraculous flower. I offered her a cookie and made her tell me the story. She swears up and down that it was a plain old mustard seed she planted, and well, I—I think . . ." Molly stammered a bit but finally blurted out, "This is not a mustard plant."

Helen was caught off guard. "Well, I know, but—it's just that—"

"Did you see the seed packet, Helen?"

"Well, of course I did. Plain as plain can be. In big black letters. 'Mustard.' At first, I thought it was a mistake, so I went to the feed store and asked Joe about it. He backed up Lila's story."

"You mean, *Joe* said it's a mustard plant?"

"No, no. He hasn't even been here to see the plant. He just told me that that he sold her mustard seeds. That's all." Helen sighed. "Molly, I don't know for sure what kind of seed Lila planted, but I've checked every seed catalogue and garden book I can find, and this plant is not in any of them. It's like it just came from, well—"

"Heaven?" asked Molly expectantly. Her slim hands gave her a saint-like authority, and her white face and brown eyes brimmed with a willingness to wonder.

Helen looked at her fondly and thought how very young she seemed, untouched by the kind of sadness that Helen herself had known. Molly was like all starry-eyed young people; ready to believe that good could come without cost. Life had taught Helen to know better, but she held her peace.

"Sure. Heaven. Why not?" she replied, and put her arm around Molly's shoulders. If hope had sprung up in her garden, and so in her child, who was she to refuse it?

Aunt Gladys came the day after Molly. She arrived at the door with a leaf-green tote slung over her shoulder. It was embroidered with a dozen colorful flowers, each labeled with its name in a flowery handwritten style. In her tote were three sizable horticulture handbooks. She had been doing her research. Helen offered to carry the bag, and Gladys readily and thankfully complied. As she handed off the tote to her host, she looked up at Helen. "I may still have two green thumbs," she said as she held both of her thumbs up in the air, "but my mind is not quite as green as it used to be." She tapped one finger on the side of her head. "I think it's time to check this plant's references, so I've brought some help. I want to find out just what it is and where it's from."

When they reached the tea table in the garden, Gladys took the books from the bag and laid them on the tabletop. Lila jumped down from her perch in the tree and ran to join them.

"Hello, my dear," Gladys began, with the friendly glance that always made Lila smile. "Your plant is looking very nice." She touched Lila lightly on the cheek. "Will you show me the bloom I've heard so much about?" Lila nodded, and they walked over to the plant. Gladys spent several minutes looking at the new red bloom and at the other buds that were just beginning to break open. Then they walked back to the table where they sat down to cold lemonade that Helen had brought from the house.

Gladys folded her hands in front of her and looked at the little girl. "Lila, dear, have you ever wondered why your tree doesn't look like the mustard plant on your seed packet?"

Lila looked at Gladys but didn't answer. The question voiced a doubt in her own mind that she had refused to acknowledge. It set her heart beating faster with anticipation, or fear.

Gladys didn't wait for an answer. "I'm an old lady, and I've been gardening since I was your age. I've seen wild mustard many times in my life, Lila. It's a small plant with a yellow bloom." She paused for a moment and considered the plant in silence. "Now, I don't know exactly what your plant is, but it's not any kind of mustard plant I've ever known. So, the question we need to ask is just what kind of plant is it? I've brought my books so we can figure it out. Is that all right with you?"

Lila nodded, quietly finished her last gulp of lemonade, and skipped back across the yard to the tree.

Helen watched, pleased to see that her little girl seemed none the worse for the conversation. She had been uncertain of what effect Gladys's inquiry might have on Lila, but for the moment, all was well. Helen stepped inside to put on the kettle and when she emerged with the tea a few minutes later, she saw a sight that set her heart at ease.

"Lila dear, it's a mystery!" Aunt Gladys's eyes glimmered as she called across the yard to where Lila sat next to the tree. "It's a real mystery. Come look at these."

Lila went to Aunt Gladys and peered down at the open book with its pictures of leaves and buds. Their two heads, one golden, one gray, bent over the pages and a hum of whispering ensued. They reveled, those two, in all they could not answer or find, and when Aunt Gladys departed, the matter of Lila's plant was no less mysterious than when the study began.

There were more mustard-tree teas. As the summer ripened and passed, it became a common occurrence for neighbors and friends to call, or just show up at the front door, asking, "Might we see the mustard tree?" While adults busied themselves with tea and chatter, Lila held her own small court in the garden with the neighborhood children. Every newcomer heard a fresh telling of the significance of mustard seeds, and the story of her tree. With dramatic flair, Lila would then bind each child to an absolute promise to guard the tree "with your very life." If their eyes were wide and their vows solemn, she condescended to let them water, or even touch, the bright little tree.

The children's mothers watched from the covered porch, rockers creaking. It was a pleasure Helen had longed for but seldom enjoyed. She was the only young widow in the neighborhood, a single mother with no extended family, who worked three days a week at the bank to make ends meet. Her life felt so difficult that she had assumed she had no time for friendship. But Lila's plant had changed that. She savored the days when the mothers came. Late afternoons after work were especially enjoyable—a golden time that lingered, minutes dripping by like honey, when the mothers of Lila's friends came by to fetch their children. "Oh, stay a minute," Helen often found herself saying. "I'll put on the kettle."

And soon, Helen too had a court all her own. Young and old, the women gathered on her porch in the evening, mouths quick with gossip, laughter swift as the swallows diving through the dusk. Aunt Gladys came often as well, perching her small frame in the biggest rocking chair and swinging her legs like a child.

Cal reigned over all as king, filling his place at the head of the table with a jolly bossiness that neither Lila nor Helen could resist. He bellowed orders for his favorite pies and cajoled his mother with pleas to stay out just a bit later, and tugged at Lila's braids whenever she was in reach. He was a consummate host, ushering each new visitor to the garden, thundering Lila's name as he went. He claimed his father's old chair in the evenings and looked as if he was growing an inch a day.

And the mustard tree grew. More blooms emerged to satisfy the steady stream of admirers. Every door in the Armstrong house stayed open that summer, ready to welcome visitors. Fireflies danced in the air and voices lingered in the old silences and it was as if the house itself and the people it sheltered were part of the garden, growing and stretching like the young tree alive with promise in their midst.

And yet, not every knock announced an admirer.

A swift volley of raps on the front door prodded Helen off the couch. They were the tight, high knocks made by the knuckles of a small hand. By now, most of Helen's friends just announced their presence at the screen door as they pulled it open. But this caller stood outside, her unsmiling face framed by the mesh of the screen.

Mrs. Boyd was the forty-something wife of a local war hero. She was tall and gaunt, always looking starved despite her husband's reputation for wealth and hers for costly tastes. She was not an unattractive woman, except for the unappealing sternness of spirit that gave her face its pinched look. To everyone, she was "Mrs. Boyd," never "Elizabeth," and she preferred it that way.

Mrs. Boyd was the only neighbor on the street who had never joined the other women on Helen's porch. Helen knew from Lila that Mrs. Boyd had come by one day while Helen was at work. She had come, looked at the plant, and left quickly without a word between her perfunctory greeting and goodbye. She was just one of many people who had come by in the same way, and now she stood on the doorstep, her thin face flushed with the afternoon heat, her coiffed hair a little awry, and her purse clutched too tightly in her gloved hands.

Helen pushed open the screen door and Mrs. Boyd barged right past her and into the foyer. Once inside, she spun around, clutched her purse even more tightly, and demanded hoarsely, "I want to see that tree again."

"Why hello, Mrs. Boyd, and of course," said Helen as nicely as she could. "It just gets more beautiful every—" Helen's words were cut short as Mrs. Boyd set off for the garden. Helen jogged to catch up, for the woman strode straight out the kitchen door and nearly ran for the tree. Fear tightened around Helen's heart as she caught up. Mrs. Boyd was already at the tree, taking a piece of paper out of her purse. Her wiry fingers grabbed at one of the leaves to examine it, and Helen felt an immediate need to protect the tree, as one would protect a child from harm. Helen cried out, "Please. Be careful!" But Mrs. Boyd had already seen all that she had come to see.

"I knew it!" She stood and glowered at Helen. "That's no mustard tree. What in the world are you thinking, Helen Armstrong? Letting Lila rave on like she does? You're letting her be a foolish girl, and you're making a fool of yourself, too."

Helen's face flushed, but she stood her ground with calm and was glad to note that she was at least an inch taller than Mrs. Boyd. "Lila is not raving. She's happy.

And what exactly is it that you know? It's certainly not a mustard plant, but that's what Lila planted. I've seen the seed packet. Whatever it is, it makes her happy, and other people too. So what has you in such a bother?"

"Oh, for heaven's sake, Helen. Stop being so naïve. Do you think an angel came down and planted some kind of celestial seed?" She forced the paper she was holding into Helen's hand. "If you want to know what that thing is, just look at this. Or do you prefer to stay ignorant?"

Helen raised the sheet and looked at it. What she saw on the crumpled paper was a photograph of a plant. She grimaced because the picture did, indeed, look like Lila's tree. It was a page ripped from a garden book about exotic plants. She silently mouthed the Latin words printed just beneath the photo: "Eu-phor-bi-a pu-ni-ce-a." She closed her eyes.

"It's one of Joe's crazy exotic plants. He collects these things like other men collect German beer steins." Mrs. Boyd was getting more agitated the more she talked about Joe. "He's got a madhouse of a garden behind that seed and feed store, and God only knows what he's got hiding in the corners of that dingy shop of his."

"Mrs. Boyd," Helen pleaded. "Elizabeth, please. Why are you so upset? It isn't hurting anyone."

Mrs. Boyd tensed. "My son Tom was here last week with a friend, and Lila told them all about the plant. Tom came home raving about a mustard seed and a miracle tree. I tried to talk some sense into him, but he wouldn't listen to me. Maybe it's nothing to you, but I don't want my son believing in this kind of nonsense." Mrs. Boyd was crimson with anger. "Now Tom wants to buy some mustard seed from Joe and plant it in *our* yard. He wants to see if it will bring his daddy home more often. He wants to grow his own *miracle*." She paused and softened for a moment, but caught herself and tensed again. "You've got the whole neighborhood believing fairy tales that no self-respecting Christian ought. I'll put a stop to it!"

Before Helen could reply, a deep voiced boomed out from the front door, "Hello?"

Helen excused herself and ran for the house, glad of the timely distraction, but Mrs. Boyd drew herself up like an offended hen and scurried along behind her, face red, hair ruffled, fairly bristling with triumph. "I beat him over here, you know," said Mrs. Boyd. "Now he can explain it to you himself."

Joe stood waiting on the front doorstep. He held his timeworn Tilley hat in his big brown hands, and his whole lean body curved as if in apology.

Before Joe could say a word, Mrs. Boyd pointed a wiry finger at him and took up her case. "He switched the seeds, Helen." She emphasized each word as if it were a dirty, terrible thing that had to be spit from her mouth. "He gave your Lila mustard seeds, but then switched them somehow." Mrs. Boyd looked at Joe with disgust. "He didn't confess in so many words, hemming and hawing like he does, but he didn't deny it when I asked him. And just how long were you going to let that little girl think she had some kind of miracle when it was all just a trick?"

Joe wasn't looking at Mrs. Boyd. His eyes were fixed on the small, square face that peered down upon him from the top of the stairs. The gaze of that face was almost more than he could bear, but he walked a step forward and held out his weathered hand. "Lila?"

The little girl ran down the stairs and stood at the bottom, her hand still on the rail. Helen moved to Lila's side and pulled her close. Lila's face was all angles, her muscles tense. "What do you mean, a trick?" She was staring at Mrs. Boyd, who turned away and spoke directly to Helen.

"So, are you going to tell her? Tell her the truth!" said Mrs. Boyd.

Helen didn't answer. She wanted desperately to cradle Lila's heart in such a way that it would not break. But the damage was already done. The secret doubt that Lila had kept hidden was out in the open.

The silence felt like a frayed rope pulled to the point of breaking. When the rope snapped, three things happened at once. Lila bolted from her mother's embrace and ran for the back door. Helen tore the page from Mrs. Boyd's garden book into several pieces, then gave Mrs. Boyd a look that would sear the very sun and said in a low voice, "Tell her the truth? Damn your truth."

Cal was the third strand of the rope. He had heard everything from the top of the stairs, and he came bounding down. He put his arms around his mother and looked at the pinch-faced woman standing before the shreds of paper on the floor. "You're wrong," he said, "and you don't understand." Cal gave his mom a tight squeeze and ran for the garden.

Mrs. Boyd left without a word. Joe stood, hat in his hands, looking down at his boots. After a few seconds he looked up at Helen, eyes dull and darkened with remorse.

"Mrs. Armstrong, I am so sorry." He spoke slowly and deliberately, as though fighting for the words to come out. "What I did was wrong. But it was not a trick. I know this isn't the time to explain. I'm sorry." Then he too turned and walked out the front door. Helen sat down on the bottom stair and put her face in her hands.

Cal caught up with Lila just as she seized her spade and swung it at the plant. "You're just a trick," she cried, "I hate you." Her blow caught the largest bloom on its short neck and left it barely hanging on the stem. Her second blow severed it. Red and gashed, it lay on the grass as Lila drew back for another blow at the plant.

"Stop! Lila, stop," Cal yelled. He grabbed her by the wrist and wrested the spade from her hand. Though the whisper of his voice could usually freeze Lila mid-step, the sound of it in her ear, with the sight of her hope and faith mutilated on the ground, only maddened her and she fought against his grip. Cal knotted her into the gentle but unyielding circle of his arms. Lila strained against him with all her strength, butting her small wild head against his chest. She flailed and sobbed, forgetting for once to treat him like a fragile thing, forgetting to hold herself back from touching him. She fought until her tears left her drained and she went limp against his chest. Cal's heart throbbed under her cheek and she relaxed in his familiar scent.

"I'm sorry, Cal," Lila whispered, and closed her eyes. "I tried."

Cal held her close, his hand stroking her hair protectively. He took her in his strong arms and stood up. Lila felt suddenly safe in the shelter of Cal's embrace. The warmth of his skin eased her, and she felt the gallop of his heart as if it would outrun any grief or pain. She could not see the sudden pallor of his face as he stepped into the house, did not feel the slight stumble that he caught with an effort that whitened his lips. He carried Lila to the staircase where their mother was still sitting, her eyes glossy with spent tears.

"I think it's high time Lila gets to enjoy the sick couch and some TLC. Don't you agree, Mama?" Helen, seeing her son taking charge, and knowing what he overcame to do so, forced a smile of approval. "Mama, you make Lila some lemonade and I'll get her settled."

Cal laid Lila gently on the overstuffed living room couch, which he knew all too well. He put the pillows under her head, grabbed their dad's old plaid camping blanket that they loved as much, and spread it over his sister. He tucked the edges under her on both sides, and left her with a brotherly pat on the head. Lila was already asleep when her mother returned with lemonade.

She woke a long while later at her mother's gentle touch. When she asked for Cal, her mother told her only that he had gone to the hospital to finish a few more tests. It would be a long time before Lila would hear how, while she slept, her mother crept upstairs to find Cal collapsed on the braided rug by his bed, Mrs. Boyd's faith-crushing pieces of paper in a savage pile of shreds, and the severed flower in his hand. The ambulance had come, this time without sirens or lights, and had quietly taken Cal from the house.

Lila stood at the front door of the house, looking out into the street. She stood in a silence so absolute she could hear the beat of her own heart, sharp and steady as the tick of the kitchen clock. The quiet brooded in and about her, hot and thick, filling up the rooms like water so that she felt she could not breathe. She was alone. Cal was gone, in the hospital with what her mother now called "a little relapse." Her mother was asleep at the kitchen table, slumped over a pile of letters and bills.

Lila hated the silence because she feared it. She could not escape her own dark thoughts. She yearned for a voice to shatter the quiet, for a knock to draw her into action, but no one came around anymore. Once Cal was sick again, and the news of Mrs. Boyd's discovery spread through the neighborhood, people stopped coming. Joe came once, tall and solemn, asking to see her, but she couldn't yet untangle how she felt about him. Today, though, she wished he'd come.

Lila meandered through the house to the back porch and looked out over the yard. The tea table sat empty. Her apple tree refuge held no appeal. And her mustard tree was dying. For the whole summer, the tree had been like a friend that reached out and gave and grew just as she asked it. But she had destroyed it. And the shame of that act was a presence she could not escape. Her heart drummed in her chest with it now and she couldn't bear the garden any longer. She ran back through the house, out the front door, and bounded into the street. It was deserted. The heat of late August sapped the verve from everything that moved, and not a soul was out of doors in the late afternoon. The trees were still, listless and drunk with heat. The scuffing of her sandals on the pavement was the only sound in the heavy air. She felt she was being watched with silent disapproval.

Lila wanted to shout, to scream, but just as she opened her mouth an unexpectedly cool wind blew into her face. The breeze was so cool, so fresh, that it caught her by surprise, and she chased it up the narrow, shady street. She ran until she was breathless and damp, blood pounding in her ears. She reached the cul-de-sac where a tiny wilderness of wood and field surrounded the prim, old houses, and she gathered her breath to run again—but a familiar voice stopped her.

"Lila?" She looked around at a small frame cottage with gables and dormers. Aunt Gladys was sitting in a rocker on the front porch. "Come see me, love." Her voice was kind but also commanding in the way of sweet but determined old women. Lila turned toward the gate, but when her hand was on the latch, she paused. Aunt Gladys's keen old eyes would see right through her soul and find her shame. She wasn't sure she could bear for anyone to see the darkness within her. She almost turned back, but the wind wouldn't let her.

This time, the cool wind was at her back, nudging her forward. She went through the gate and found herself in a garden paradise—plants of every kind, shrubs, ivy, ferns, flowers, green and colorful things like paintings in a storybook, reached toward her. The tall, fully crowned trees on both sides of the garden still had summer leaves on them, and they cast a dappled shade over every part of the little park. As Lila climbed the ten steps up to the covered porch, she was greeted by yet another sea of plants—hanging baskets of flowers, potted plants at every step and in every kind of decorated pot. The breeze played a song of welcome through a set of wind chimes as she wound through the greenery toward Aunt Gladys. Lila understood why she was considered the best gardener in town. The old woman beamed as she got closer and patted the seat beside her. Lila squirmed into it and held tight to the chair's arms.

"Now, Lila, tell me all about it, dear," Aunt Gladys said, without any offer of small talk. She combed Lila's long golden hair with her gentle fingers. "Everything. Start to finish."

And Lila did. She didn't mean to at first, but the words spilled from her, chasing each other out of her heart in a torrent of release. She spat out Mrs. Boyd's harsh words, and remembered Joe's sad voice. She bewailed the friends who came no more, and the laughter that was gone, and Cal sick in the hospital. As she spoke, the tight place in her chest that had ached for days began to feel spacious and clean again. But a last blistered corner still throbbed within her because she could not bring herself to confess what she had done to her tree. She finished her story in tears.

"It wasn't a miracle," Lila sobbed, "and Cal's sick again and everybody knows I was wrong."

Aunt Gladys took her hand, squeezing it with affection. Lila snuggled up to her, about to relax in her compassion until the old woman's words set her upright.

"But Lila, what's really changed?"

Lila's face puckered. "What's changed? Well, just everything!" Lila pulled herself away and crossed her arms. "I just told you. Cal's sick, the tree wasn't real, and everybody knows it."

"Yes, I know dear. But Cal was better for a while, wasn't he?"

"But he's sick again, so it didn't work. The mustard tree was just a trick. A big, fat fake."

"Ahh, but how do you know that for sure?" said Aunt Gladys. "That tree of yours is a beauty! Maybe it's not a mustard tree, but it's a rare wonder. You planted a mustard seed with faith and you got something else. It's a gift, you see, no matter how it got there."

Lila squirmed. Her heart throbbed. She didn't want to tell Aunt Gladys what she had done to her gift, but she knew if she didn't tell she might be ill.

"I hurt the tree, Aunt Gladys. I cut off its branch because it wasn't a miracle and I was mad. I haven't watered it and it's dying."

So the hot, poisonous truth that had burned and blistered her heart was told. But with its confession, the fire of her disappointment died down too, and to Lila's surprise, she felt better, not worse. She sighed, and felt that she had not taken so deep and clean a breath for a long time. Glancing up, she caught Aunt Gladys's approving smile.

"Here, love." Gladys offered her a bowl of red and white candies. "Have a peppermint. They clear the mind."

Lila gingerly took only one candy since that's what her mother had taught her. But the bowl wasn't withdrawn after she had, so she took another. Both went into her mouth and the sharp sweetness filled her as she rolled the candies around with her tongue.

"Lila." Gladys leaned down close. "The trouble isn't with your tree or even in what you did to it. The trouble is that you let Elizabeth Boyd's words turn your tree into a trick instead of the gift it was meant to be." Gladys set the candy bowl on the table and leaned back in her rocker. "All that Boyd woman proved was that your tree wasn't a mustard plant. Fine. But she was wrong about everything else. She made you think it was all just a trick, so it couldn't be a miracle, and you believed her."

"But it *was* a trick," said Lila, trying to sound earnest and finding it difficult with a mouth full of candy.

"You can call what Joe did a trick," Aunt Gladys said, "or you can call it a gift. The choice is yours. But whatever you choose to call it, that tree of yours is a wonder, child."

Lila sucked on her candy and looked at Gladys with puzzlement. "Well, then how do you know what's a miracle and what's not?"

"You take every good thing that comes your way as a gift, Lila. Every single thing," She spoke in a strong voice of sudden depth. She stood up from the rocker, her joints stiff from arthritis but her eyes as steady and clear as a child's. Picking up her carved wooden cane, she walked to the porch rail and looked out on her garden and the tall, wind-tossed trees. "Faith isn't getting everything you ask for, child.

That's not what the story about the mustard tree meant. Faith means hoping. Faith means living as if one day everything broken will be made better and seeing every good thing as a promise that it will. Your tree, Joe's gift, came to you because you had faith. But it was just a beginning, Lila. You have to keep on hoping."

"But I hurt it," Lila whispered, "and it might die."

"Hurts can heal, child." Aunt Gladys turned to face Lila, and spoke to her firmly with bright, challenging eyes. "And you can help to heal them. Water that tree again. Let it grow. Let your wonder grow again, and hope will be its fruit. It's a beautiful thing, your mustard tree."

"But everyone knows it's not a miracle, Aunt Gladys. And I don't know if Cal will get better." Lila frowned.

"Sweet girl, you can't live by doubt. You can't live by maybes or fears. If you're going to live at all you have to live by hope. That means deciding that Joe's gift and your faith and all the joy this summer are the real things and the cancer and fear are shadows that will one day pass. I don't know what will happen with your Cal. But I know that God gave you a mighty gift in that tree. He let you make Cal laugh, and he helped you make your mama happy again."

Lila sighed, but nodded. Then she gave a sharp little glance at Aunt Gladys. "But what if nobody else sees it that way?"

Aunt Gladys smiled. "You teach them how to see. You can't stop the doubters any more than you can catch the wind and put it in a cage. But they can't stop you either. And if you keep on hoping you can rise right above their doubts and fly where they can't ever catch you."

Aunt Gladys pulled Lila up from the rocker and declared, "Now, let's go water that tree of yours."

Lila drew in a deep breath of the wind, and it rushed through her entire body, clean and cool. She held Aunt Gladys's hand and the two of them walked down the path through the verdant, colorful garden. Their steps quickened. Lila's heart beat faster. And the wind sang all around them as they went.

At first, it seemed the little tree might be finished. When Lila and Gladys arrived in the garden they found a shriveled thing with branches awry and leaves limp. The wounded branch jutted harshly away from the rest and all the other blooms had lost their petals. Lila knelt and stroked the tree's slim branches, patting the dirt at its base with gentle, apologetic fingers, collecting the fallen petals into a pile. Working together, Lila and Aunt Gladys fetched a full watering pail and soaked the ground around the tree. But despite their efforts, the wounded plant still looked forlorn, a leafless lost cause. Lila pursed her lips and stood up abruptly, hands on her hips. "I'm going to get Joe. He'll know what to do."

As Lila headed for the garden gate, Gladys smiled and made her way to the house. A few minutes later, bleary-eyed and bewildered, Helen lifted her head from the stack of bills on the kitchen table to find a fresh cup of tea and a friendly face. A cool breeze blew in the window.

Lila swung open the shop door and headed straight for the checkout counter.

"You've got to help me, Joe. My tree is dying 'cause I didn't water it and you've got to help me save it." Then she added, "I hurt it, Joe, and I'm sorry."

"Oh. Lila. I—I'm sorry too." He opened his big, dirt-stained hands in a gesture of apology. "I didn't mean to trick you. I mean I didn't want to trick you. I—"

"It's okay. It's a beautiful tree and I love it. Will you come help me?"

Joe rocked back on his heels and a smile began to cover his face. He hadn't expected this. He thought he'd broken Lila's trust and severed their bond of friendship. But she was back. And they were friends. And she was the girl he remembered.

Joe packed his leather bag full of tools for making things grow and then he and Lila were out the door. They marched through the streets without speaking, and just as dusk was pooling under the trees and hushing the sky they entered the garden through the back gate.

Joe knelt in the grass, opened his bag, and set to work. Gently, he clipped the jagged branch so that the cut was clean and smooth. He propped the weary branches on wooden stilts that held them straight. He loosened the soil around the tree and sprinkled it with a powdery and seedy mix. When Lila asked what it was, he told her with a mysterious smile that it was "good medicine." Then they watered the tree once more, gave a pat to the damp ground, and stood.

"That's all we can do for now," Joe said. He put his tools back in his bag and secured it with its old buckle-style leather straps. "Be sure to give it a little water every day. And if something doesn't seem right, you come tell me. Good evening to your mother." And he left.

That night, the house was filled with laughter again. Aunt Gladys cooked a hearty stew of potatoes, carrots, onions, and summer squash in a rich tomato stock. Helen baked a fresh loaf of bread, and they ate it slathered in butter and honey. They lingered on the porch as the shadows grew, sipping sweet tea, talking late into the summer evening. And when they finally turned to face the darkened house, they found that the rooms felt warm and full of welcome.

Lila and her mother called Cal at the hospital that night. He was in good spirits. Lila checked on her tree once before bedtime. She believed it would grow now. Even as she climbed into her bed, and her mother tucked her safely under the covers and turned out her light, she no longer feared waking to the two o'clock dream of sirens and lights. Out in the garden, the brave tree was fighting to live again, and she felt it, a gracious presence in the shadows. She slept easily that night, with the cool wind drifting over her face.

Lila settled into a new, late-summer rhythm of days. Perhaps it was the impending fall of autumn that slowed her down. She no longer kept an anxious vigil for the tree. She was content to water, to watch, and to wait. She was happy simply to lie in the cool grass of the garden in deep and thoughtful silence. Every day, Lila went with her mother to visit Cal in the hospital. She sat on his bed and told him how the tree was perking up and beginning to heal and look like its old self—branches holding straight without help, leaves plumping back to life in the sun, a last bloom working hard to open before summer's end. Cal was not back to his old self, but Lila loved to see his smile when she regaled him with details.

The neighborhood children began to visit again. Lila welcomed the sight and sound of her friends. She was gentler now, savoring the simple fact of laughter and friendship each afternoon. She no longer required that they bind themselves to an oath of protection. They played and talked and the tree was no longer the subject of everyone's attention. Except for Tom Boyd. For him, the tree was still the center and wonder of each visit.

Tom was a thin child of deep quiet. Lila had never really known him before, but late that summer he became a true friend. It was Tom Boyd who seemed to have taken on the mantle of the plant's protector, probably with his mother's stern disapproval—though she never mentioned the matter again. Whenever Tom came, he spent most of his time watching over the tree and checking it for healing and growth. And on the last day of August, it was Tom who made the great discovery. "Lila!" His high, cracking voice shattered the quiet of the early morning. "Come look!"

Tom was on his hands and knees, his nose to the ground at the base of the tree. Lila knelt beside him and looked. And there she in the damp, rich soil she saw a tiny colony of green sprouts pushing up from the earth. Not just one or two, but a whole clump. She gently touched the shoots; they were strong and healthy.

Neither child knew what the new growth might be, nor from where it could have come. But Lila knew what to do. She threw open the back gate, and ran straight for the seed store. Joe was just opening for business as Lila grabbed his hand and insisted that he come "Right now!" Joe assured her he would be along shortly and urged her to go make sure the birds didn't eat the tender shoots for breakfast.

When Joe arrived he found both children lying prone, studying the new sprouts. He chuckled as he knelt beside them.

"What is this, Joe? Are these weeds? Are they dangerous?"

Joe put a finger under one of the sprouts. "Well, Lila, I reckon it's just what you ordered. These are mustard greens."

Lila's eyes got wide. Then she laughed. Her mirth infected Joe, then Tom, until they were all in an uproar. After all the to-do and confusion, real mustard plants had finally sprouted!

When Joe and Tom had left, Lila lay flat on her stomach to stare at the seedlings. She wished they could talk to her, tell her where they came from, why they were here. But this, she realized, was a mystery, almost more of a miracle than the tree itself had been.

And so Lila hatched a new plan in her mind. One late afternoon, she took her spade in one hand and two small clay pots in the other. Carefully, she dug good soil from the garden and filled the pots. Then with cautious fingers, she formed a hole in the center of each and took them over to her tree. Just as she pressed her spade into the mustard sprout colony, Tom Boyd came up from behind her.

"Lila, what are you doing?" he cried. "You aren't going to dig them all up, are you?"

"Nope," Lila calmly replied as she worked the spade into the earth. "Just a couple of them." She eased a clump of mustard out of the ground and gently set it into the hole in one of the pots, tamping down the soil around it. Then she took the other pot and did the same.

"I planted one mustard seed for Cal and it finally grew," she said to Tom. "It's kind of a miracle, so I'm taking it to him. I think it will help him remember to be glad even while he's in the hospital."

Tom knelt beside Lila. "But what are you going to do with the second pot? Is it for your mother?"

"Nope," chirped Lila. "It's for you." She picked up the small pot and handed it to a very surprised Tom Boyd. "You need some mustard of your own," she said.

At that moment, Helen stepped out onto the back porch. "Are you ready, Lila?" she called. "Cal will be getting tired if we don't get there soon."

"Ready!" Lila called back. She smiled at Tom, whose eyes brimmed with a gladness she had not seen there before, and then she ran for the porch.

As she looked back and waved goodbye to Tom, he called out, "Come see my plant when you can. Bye."

Helen looked at the pot in Lila's hands and raised a questioning eyebrow at her daughter. "It's for Cal. You'll see." Lila walked to the car in a mysterious and determined silence. She didn't say a word on the ride to the hospital. She just followed her mother up the stairs and into the small, green-walled room where Cal was propped on a bed.

Lila held her breath, as she always did going into Cal's room. Cal was frail from the treatments, but his face stretched into its old grin at sight of Lila. His thick, dark hair was in its usual mess. He winked and made a special effort to sit up in his bed. "Hey, squirt. What's that?" he asked, pointing to the pot in her hands. Lila cleared a place on his bedside table and set the little pot down with a ceremonial flourish. Then she jumped up onto his bed and gave him a tight hug around the neck.

"Cal," she breathed, her voice taut with excitement, "the mustard finally grew. That's what the plant is!"

Cal gave a low whistle, picked up the pot, and examined it. He touched the little leaves with reverent fingers and bent close to Lila. "Well what do you know? After all this time, the wonders keep on coming." He tousled her hair and they laughed. "Is this really the mustard you planted?"

"I don't know," Lila said matter-of-factly, then her voice softened, "but Aunt Gladys says that every good thing is a promise that one day everything will be right again. So it's for you. It's a promise." Her voice was tender and low as she watched her fragile, precious brother.

"Hey, I kept your other gift too, you know." He reached for a book on the table and opened it to the middle. "Hold out your hand."

Cal carefully removed a single pressed bloom from between the pages and gently laid it in Lila's open palm. The petals were a vibrant red, the center a splash of brilliant gold. It was the bloom she had severed from the plant in her anger and grief. Now she saw it as a beautiful thing. A hopeful thing.

"You must have a green thumb, little sister, 'cause you're pretty good at growing miracle plants." Lila smiled as he took the bloom from her and carefully put it back in the fold of the book. "But Lila," he said, sinking back against the pillows. "You're the real wonder."

Lila held his hand as he took a deeper breath and rested for a while. Her mother sat beside her on the bed, and the three of them were still in the honeyed, late-day quiet. Cal's eyes closed for a few minutes of sleep, and for an instant, Lila's heart leapt in fear at sight of his thin, weary face. But she turned. The little mustard plant sat bravely on the bedside table, its leaves already tilting toward the window and the gold of the sunset. Lila took a deep breath and closed her eyes and did her best to live by hope.

Sapling

by Andrew Peterson

It rained for days, and heavy wind
Bent the cherry sapling over,
Stakes yanked out and the twine untied
From the thumb and fragile fingers
Of its trunk and first young branches.

I walked out today to tell it
I'd do my best to help it grow
Old and straight and tall. My boots squished
In the high grass all the way down
From the house to the lower field.

When I got to the poor, young tree,
I put a hand on the gray bark
And knew, at once, that I'm the one,
The naked one in need of help.
As I grow old, the tree grows tall;

The roots grow down; they eat and drink
In the cold, wet dark, which does not—
Cannot—thwart the strong, patient life,
The rising up, the reaching deep:
Lovely storm-blown branch, steady root.

Ash Wednesday

by Rebecca Reynolds

Today I knelt to watch the genuflection of the honeybee.
Her little face was buried in the virgin flush of spring,
at her knees, coffers of gold, weighted with promise.

Perhaps a hundred times she dove into the crocus,
dove, rose,
dove, drank,
dove, nuzzled out savors of glory,
dove, wings a-flurry,
dove,
  hovered,
  resisted,
  remembered,
  unable to refuse such bounty
dove,
dove,
dove,
dove, enveloped among the indigos,
silk upon silk upon silk.

If her tiny chest beats not wild with praise,
mine will sound for us both,
for men throw branches upon ruined streets shouting, "Make way,"
when they have no such intention at all.

Yet, the Messiah rides on the back of a donkey,
and on the stripes of the honeybee.
Blessed is she who comes in the name of the Lord.

Flying Home from Brooklyn

by Andrew Peterson

We spent a day in the city,
And I thought, as I always do,
How I would like to live there
In Brooklyn, maybe, or Queens,
Manhattan—a square foot or two.

I nurse the thought for a while
That I'd be a better writer,
A better poet, better man,
If I sank in the quick river
Of bodies and buses and blunders,

Of traffic and taxis and wonders,
And swam upstream through New York,
An even smaller fish at play
In an even bigger sea.
I'd wear a black coat and strut,

Speak up and out, assert myself
Like the man I might have been,
Eat at fine establishments,
Pull on gleaming leather gloves
To hail the cabs, or tip my cap,

At fellow writers hunching
Over cocktails and staring
Sadly at their happiness
Reflected in the window glass.
Later, in a little corner

Of a little third floor flat
At a little wooden desk,
I sit with something steaming
In a mug beside my laptop.
I'd sit for hours and lonely hours,

An oasis: quiet, calm
Amidst the honking, screeching,
Wasteland of possible roads.
Words would bustle from the pen
Like commuters from the train,

To speed along the pages lined,
Little lives on crowded streets.
"Welcome," I'd say to the words,
"To the greatest city in the world.
Let me show you around, my friends."

Then I think of our house in the hills
That hug the Cumberland River.
Green and golden light rises
Like mist around me. I am swinging
On the porch, the children come

Scrabbling out of the warm woods
At the first drops of rain, laughing
In the old language of creature
Made immortal, so alive
In the tremulous tension

Of all the holy power
Of a million singing suns
Loomed into strands of ether glow
Weaved into the essential cloth
Of broken woman, broken man.

As the storm rattles the windows,
Bends the limbs of honey locust,
The children toss their walking sticks
In the grass and stomp up the steps,
Slam the door, a noisy stampede

Of angel horses. The daylight
Drops down from the rain-dark clouds,
Hides in the house with the children.
I move inside because the rain
Is cooling the tops of my feet,

And I ready my trusty pen,
There in the little corner
Of the little room, my little desk—
Oh, this oasis of calm
In this city of tree and child,

Where bird and bough rest in the blessing
Of rain and rain, this holy rain.
Alas, I find it just as hard
To write (but just as easy, too)
As it would have been in Brooklyn.

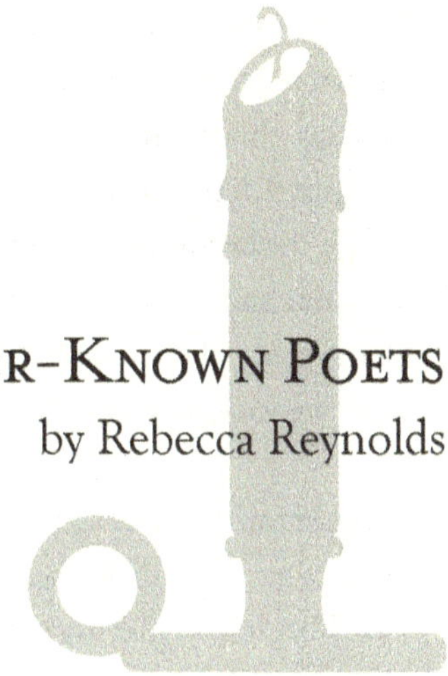

The Constitution of Lesser-Known Poets

by Rebecca Reynolds

I would rather walk alone
than join some alliance
promising to name me.

For the inclination of a label
is constriction,
and I am not inclined to temper
explorations.

I would rather live meagerly than gain notoriety
by dancing like a circus dog
turning pretty, skirted tricks.

I would rather not be published,
not be accepted,
I would rather write without readers,
wander in the thick luxury of obscurity,
than be lauded by the mighty of our time.
(I have seen whom the mighty laud.)

Give me instead an audience
of two quiet children
who are thoughtful.
I would delight them, if I could.
Or let me be loved by a widow
who has known all the pain of the world
in the space of two small, gray rooms
and twenty long years.

I would rather make imperfect sentences
than come to think so highly of myself
that I begin to value my own words
above an idea given to me.

I would write too fool often
and too fool common.
Like some common fool, I would write
knowing good and well
that scarcity enhances awe.

I would risk speaking over-plain to the mighty,
knowing they will think me a simpleton.

I would risk confounding the scientist
with stories of fairyland.
I would risk confounding the laureate
with the chemical cadence of cellular division.

I would disappoint every dignitary,
and every friend,
and every hero,

to write that one thing
that would burn me alive
if it were left uncaptured.

I would play the agnostic to the certain
and proselytize with all my heart
deep down in that black earth-side of hell
where whiskey drinkers revel.
(How I love them.)

If I sense something makes you uncomfortable,
I will do more of it.

I will fail on purpose,
defy you,
spel poorly,
conclude irresponsibly,
and make a wide pink fool of myself
rather than drink that poison
of pleasing you
for the sake of pleasing me.

For this is the way a poem begins,
and in this way love begins also.

hippochondriac: *n.* one who pretends to be a sick horse

Dear Students

by Rebecca Reynolds

My dream for you
has very little to do with grades
or test scores.

Alone, they are nothing.
They are marks on a page
that filter into systems
where marks on a page
define too much.

For the future I have seen
is vast and wild,
and percentages can no more capture
what I have seen in you
than a formula of light years
can capture the glory of a distant sun
spinning blue and gold
in that cold, far silence
where angels dance.

My fear for you
has little to do with those raw things
people your age tend to think aloud.

On the contrary, I am thankful that you are defiant
of convention for convention's sake,
of a flat, white, faux-Jesus,
of insufficient answers,
of the same old music,
and the same old new music,
of laughing too little,
of sitting in chairs indoors,
of books without heart,
of lives without passion
or adventure.

I am thankful because these things tell me
that you have not let the drowsy drone of earth
quell your newborn scream.
You are unsatisfied,
as you should be,
with these clay-bound earth-breaths.
Be so always.

But these are my grievances:
you do not realize how beautiful you are,
or how powerful,
or how loved.

You have given up too soon
on yourselves.

You have allowed all these years of
flat, red marks on flat, white pages
to name you,
and you ask me to nod
while you toss out words
and scratch at equations,
absently,
half-heartedly.

This I will not do.
For I have heard your true names
whispered by the great Lion,
Who has spoken distant suns into being.

He has shown me
the manner of royalty you are,
men and women created for greatness.

I will expect nothing less.

toom: *n.* a place reserved for burial of the animated dead

What Jimmy Abegg Taught Me About Art

by Andrew Peterson

"As long as you're making
something," Jimmy told me,
"Then failure is a word
That has no meaning."
And so, I wrote this poem.

elephonic: *adj.* extremely large and incredibly noisy

This Is for All the Lonely Writers

by Jennifer Trafton

She sat in the second row amidst a noisy gaggle of fourth graders. She was petite and olive-skinned, and her dark eyes measured me as I paced back and forth and pontificated about matter ethereal and authorial. I could tell, from her sharp, sensitive answers to my questions, that stories were seared into her soul, branding her for a calling that perhaps even she did not yet recognize.

After her classmates had exhausted their inquiries about my writing, my age, my dog's name, and the magical source of all ideas, she quietly raised her hand:

"When you were our age, were you ever lonely?"

Her eyes were so direct, her question stated so simply and honestly, that it was perfectly clear what she was asking: Were you ever like me? Is it possible to feel so alone, so different from everyone else, and still grow up to be the kind of someone I want to be?

I couldn't, in that room full of a hundred children, run to her and throw my arms around her. And I doubted very much that she was the only one who harbored such a question in her heart. So I answered her as simply and directly as she had asked: "Yes. Yes, I was lonely. I was so shy and quiet that boys would tease me in order to see who could get me to talk. And yet in my books I found friends. As I read and wrote stories, I became other people, I went on adventures, and I found out more about who I was."

I wanted to tell her: *The loneliness will end. You will find your place.*

I wanted to tell her: *The world is full of lonely people, and someone else is looking for the friend that only you can be.*

But those are only half-truths. It would have broken my heart to speak the whole truth to her or to the nine-year-old version of myself that I saw in her eyes: *You will continue to be lonely for a long time, and your loneliness is the furnace in which fine metal will be forged, and out of that place of inner fire will rise your art. For you will be a writer someday, and words will come from those places in you where speech is muffled and still.*

I have no idea what it is like to be an outgoing, extroverted writer. I can only speak from the perspective of someone who scores 99% on the introvert scale—who still, after having had many so many dear friends in my life, pushes constantly against a wall of shyness, who still feels lonely in the midst of loving community. I'm not sure I'll ever get over the feeling of being the Picassoesque face in every crowd—slightly disjointed, slightly askew, poised on the edge of normal but too cockeyed to be cool. You would like me, surely, if only my left ear were not hanging crookedly off the end of my tongue.

But along this introverted journey I have learned a thing or two about loneliness and community and art.

When I was four years old, my pre-school teacher told my parents never to let me close myself up in my room by myself—because she could already see the tendency in me to get lost in my own mind, to bury myself in my imagination. (My parents didn't tell me about this conversation until I was an adult. Growing up, I assumed it was a universal rule that children were not allowed to close the doors of their bedrooms.) That teacher was prescient; she saw the warning signs of a lifelong struggle.

I had no right to be a lonely child. My family was extremely close and unfailingly supportive. I did not *look* different from my peers or even *act* much different (except for being quiet). The real problem was that I was too deep for my own skin. I was always standing apart from the world, analyzing it, taking it in, mulling over it. My thoughts, questions, fears, and dreams were buried so far under the surface that I did not know how to scale that chasm back to the land of other people again. It was like pulling a heavy bucket of words up from the bottom of a well; there was just too much. It was too hard.

Sometime around age thirteen, I discovered the following poem in a literature textbook:

A noiseless patient spider,
I mark'd where on a little promontory it stood isolated,
Mark'd how to explore the vacant vast surrounding,
It launch'd forth filament, filament, filament, out of itself,
Ever unreeling them, ever tirelessly speeding them.
And you O my Soul where you stand,
Surrounded, detached, in measureless oceans of space,
Ceaselessly musing, venturing, throwing, seeking the spheres to connect them,
Till the bridge you will need be form'd, till the ductile anchor hold,
Till the gossamer thread you fling catch somewhere, O my Soul.

I didn't know who Walt Whitman was. I had to look up *promontory*, *filament*, *ductile*, and *gossamer* in the dictionary. But I knew that this poem was about me, as surely as if my name had been written at the top. I was that spider. The poem expressed precisely how it felt to grow up as a shy, overly thoughtful girl. I hugged it to my heart all through high school.

And then, in college, my favorite professor told me something that was the complementary truth to my pre-school teacher's warning: "The time you spend alone with your books and your art is not wasted, and it is not selfish. That solitary learning and growing will make you a better friend, a better wife, a better mother, a better teacher." This acknowledgment and affirmation of my introversion, like the Whitman poem, made me start thinking about aloneness as the necessary fire that launches us into community.

I have heard so many people make fine distinctions between solitude and loneliness, saying that in the solitude of creativity we are alone but not lonely. Because of course solitude is the incubator of a writer, or any artist. It forces you to develop a rich interior life. The mastering of an art—and the nurturing of those disciplines of contemplation from which art grows—requires vast amounts of "alone time." Stories and poems emerge from silence. Their birthplace is a quiet gasp of wordless wonder.

Except that so often the solitude of art-making is lonely. Deeply, painfully lonely. And I think somehow it must be, to a certain extent. If you are an artist by nature, then art comes out of that place in you that cannot be shared with another human being except in this creative form. It gives a voice to inner things that otherwise could not be spoken, inner things that make you who you are in your truest moments. Flannery O'Connor said, "The quality of the novel I write will derive precisely from the peculiarity or aloneness, if you will, of the experience I write from." *Peculiarity and aloneness.* Don't most of us feel that way? And yet this sense of disjointedness and isolation can be the very source of the peculiar word that we alone can speak. If we were perfectly "normal," perfectly loved, perfectly understood, perfectly aligned with the contours of the world we find ourselves occupying, would there be anything left to say?

There comes a time in our childhood or adolescence when we learn that the world is broken. Not only that, but *we* are broken, like Humpty Dumpty, and we cannot put ourselves back together again, even when we are surrounded by well-meaning royal helpers. Loneliness is the gaping hunger of the cracks.

But the grace of art is that it thrives in broken soil. And that is why, when I saw that fourth-grade girl, full of loneliness and imagination, I saw the seedling of an artist. I saw someone who, like me, had a secret room inside. Who probably, like me, was longing for someone else to come and fill it. But no, I thought as I looked at her, seeing my own nine-year-old self, if another human being could come into that inner room and fill it up, you would stay there forever, never emerging from the cocoon of your own dreams. The fact that no one can come into that room, but you still need to share it, forces you take the precious things in that room with you and leave it—and that is a creative process, a movement outward.

It launch'd forth filament, filament, filament, out of itself...

Here is the paradox: You cannot make art except by being alone, and yet you cannot be an artist in isolation. Along with that wonder born in solitude comes an irrepressible urge to turn to someone else and tell him or her about it. The creative impulse in you speaks two things. First: *Make this.* Then: *Share this.* Do not hold it tightly to your chest. Cast it out of you and let it fall. Then cast it out again, and again, *Till the bridge you will need be form'd, till the ductile anchor hold.*

I have come to believe that in order for art to be art, it must be *given*: creativity is at its heart an act of self-giving, and it is given in gratitude for having received something. It is an act requiring great courage—courage to stand in that lonely place and at the same time to be conscious that one is surrounded by faces, and to be constantly reaching out of the loneliness into communion with the world. Art is always reaching.

Here is a further paradox: In order to *not* be alone you must go by the way of aloneness. In order to find one who can receive your words you must have the courage to first send those words on the journey out of your self into a world that may not receive them. You must *fling* that gossamer thread out across those oceans of space—and *flinging* is not a safe, calculated movement. It is reckless abandon. It is a motion of both carelessness and joy.

And you will be rejected. You will find yourself, sometimes, in community (because it is still *community* whether you like it or not, whether you are happy or not) with people who are utterly different from you, who have opposite interests and concerns, who do not understand you and whom you do not understand, and yet they could be the very people from whom you will learn the most, who will hone the edges of your spirit until it grows gentler in the friction, and to whom you must learn to give yourself because that is when the gift is hardest and riskiest and therefore valuable in its frailty.

The loneliness from which your art arises may give you insight into some deep empty place in the heart of humanity, and your unique expression of that need might be the mirror in which others can finally see themselves and know they are not alone. So by forming the fruits of our solitude into words or pictures or music, we turn loneliness into love. That work of art—that story—that poem—becomes a third place, outside of my heart and yours, yet bridging both.

My husband Pete says he could not have written his novels about Fin Button today, because marriage has taken away so much of the emptiness and sadness that was the fuel for that story. Yet how many thousands of people has he unwittingly loved through that story spun in a bachelor's empty room? I was single until I was 36, and the years leading up to marriage were pockmarked by moments of searing loneliness that will always remain part of my own peculiar experience. The gossamer thread that finally caught and held to another person was art. I offered my story—the story that had pulled me out of myself and into the world—to one particular (and equally peculiar) man. He offered his story to me. And those words wrought in our separate solitudes became the first bridge between us.

But even in marriage, even in the midst of likeminded community, even when we finally find those people who will shelter us from the burning glare of the great *alone*, we (at least we introverted artists—I cannot speak for anyone else) always ebb back into a solitary hidden place inside that is only ours, that we cannot explain to anyone, that no one else seems to see or understand, and yet we are so driven to share it that it must come out in artistic expression. This place is the spring in the mountains from which flows the river that will bless all of those precious people in our lives. It is the place of prayer, and it is the place of art. Because in that innermost place we are most aware of the things that transcend us.

Is it possible to create from a place of fullness, joy, belovedness, and belonging? I am sure there must be, but I don't know what the art of perfect wholeness looks like, because as far as I'm aware no broken person on this broken earth has ever made it. I don't know what songs Humpty Dumpty will sing when he is put back together again, yet I wonder if even then the quality of his art will derive precisely from the peculiarity of the cracks from which he was healed.

I have been deeply lonely in my life, and I have been deeply loved. And I would not part with either of those experiences, for they both have been necessary to set me upon the journey I've taken.

And so this is all I want to say to her, in the end—to the beautiful dark-eyed girl who stands on a solitary promontory, spinning her gossamer thread:

Fling your silken soul far out into the world, little spider. It will catch.

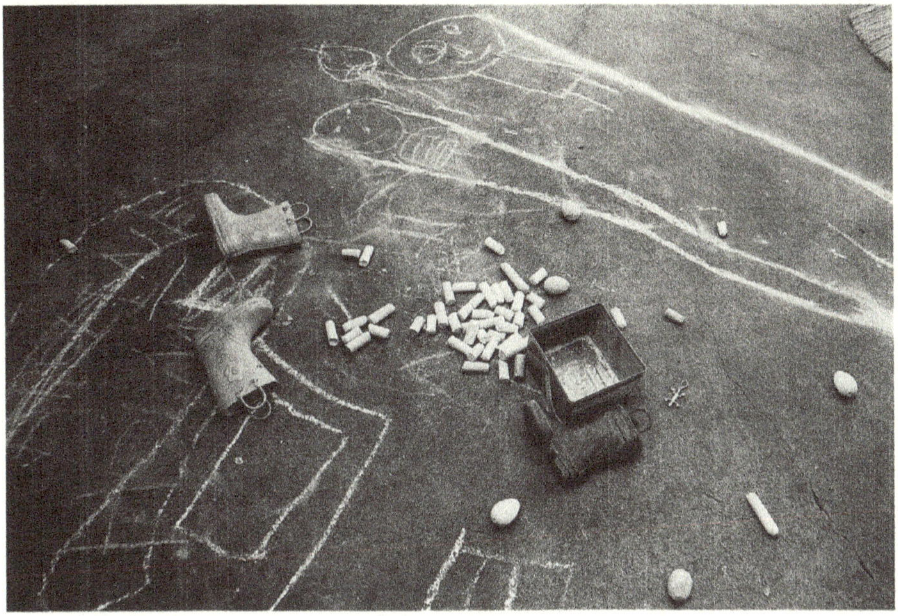

Chalk Drawings

by Eric Peters

The child's mother asked her not to empty the container of chalk onto the pavement. The girl did so anyway. She did it not to be disobedient, but because that's what she and the smiling Trinity wanted, this act of emptying.

spoothe: *v.* to give comfort with a small scooping utensil

Bartleby

By Jonny Jimison

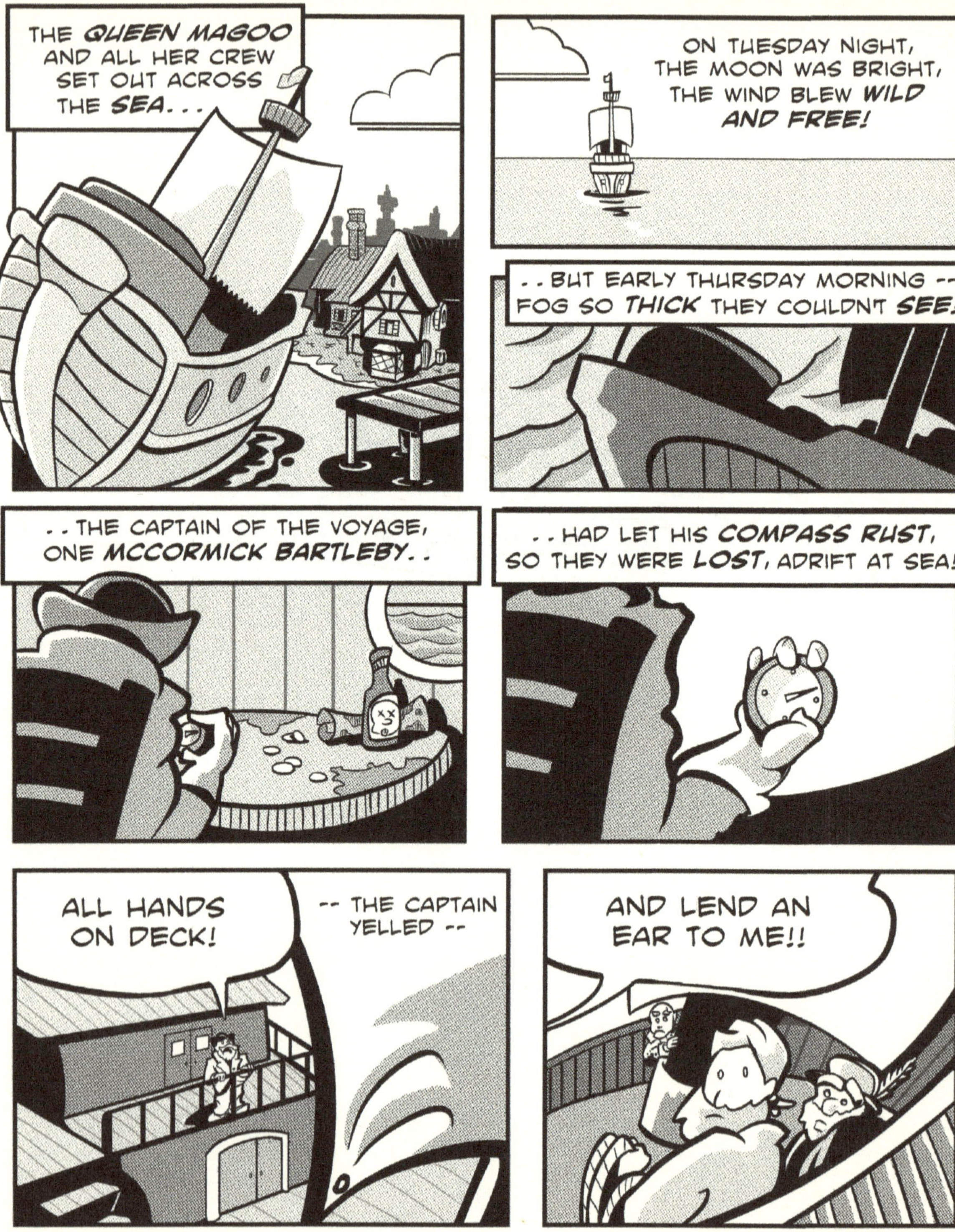
THE QUEEN MAGOO AND ALL HER CREW SET OUT ACROSS THE SEA...
ON TUESDAY NIGHT, THE MOON WAS BRIGHT, THE WIND BLEW WILD AND FREE!
..BUT EARLY THURSDAY MORNING -- FOG SO THICK THEY COULDN'T SEE!
..THE CAPTAIN OF THE VOYAGE, ONE MCCORMICK BARTLEBY..
..HAD LET HIS COMPASS RUST, SO THEY WERE LOST, ADRIFT AT SEA!
ALL HANDS ON DECK!
-- THE CAPTAIN YELLED --
AND LEND AN EAR TO ME!!

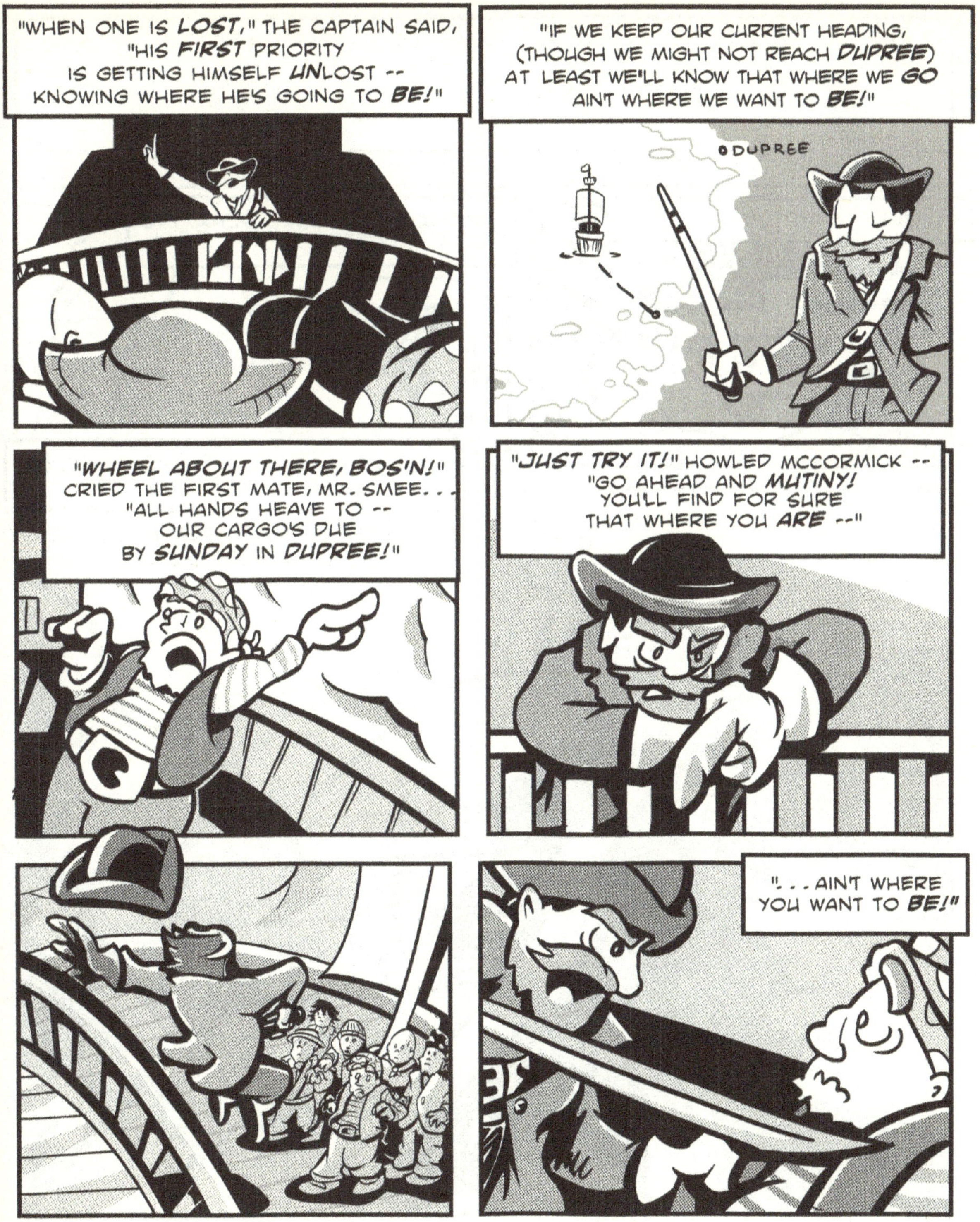
"WHEN ONE IS LOST," THE CAPTAIN SAID, "HIS FIRST PRIORITY IS GETTING HIMSELF UNLOST -- KNOWING WHERE HE'S GOING TO BE!"
"IF WE KEEP OUR CURRENT HEADING, (THOUGH WE MIGHT NOT REACH DUPREE) AT LEAST WE'LL KNOW THAT WHERE WE GO AIN'T WHERE WE WANT TO BE!"
DUPREE
"WHEEL ABOUT THERE, BOS'N!" CRIED THE FIRST MATE, MR. SMEE. . . "ALL HANDS HEAVE TO -- OUR CARGO'S DUE BY SUNDAY IN DUPREE!"
"JUST TRY IT!" HOWLED MCCORMICK -- "GO AHEAD AND MUTINY! YOU'LL FIND FOR SURE THAT WHERE YOU ARE --"
". . . AIN'T WHERE YOU WANT TO BE!"

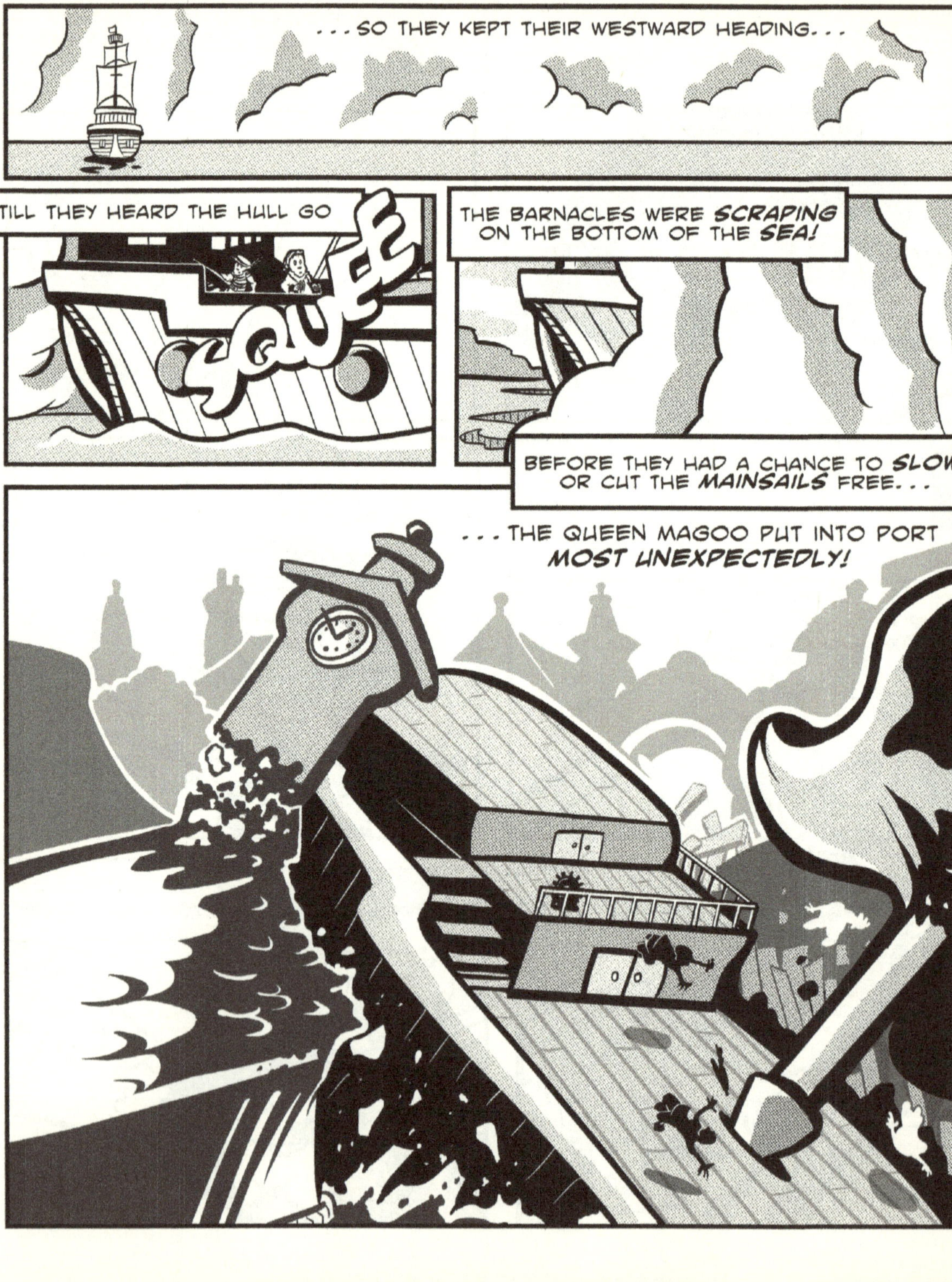
. . . SO THEY KEPT THEIR WESTWARD HEADING. . .
'TILL THEY HEARD THE HULL GO
SQUEE
THE BARNACLES WERE *SCRAPING* ON THE BOTTOM OF THE *SEA!*
BEFORE THEY HAD A CHANCE TO *SLOW* OR CUT THE *MAINSAILS* FREE. . .
. . . THE QUEEN MAGOO PUT INTO PORT *MOST UNEXPECTEDLY!*

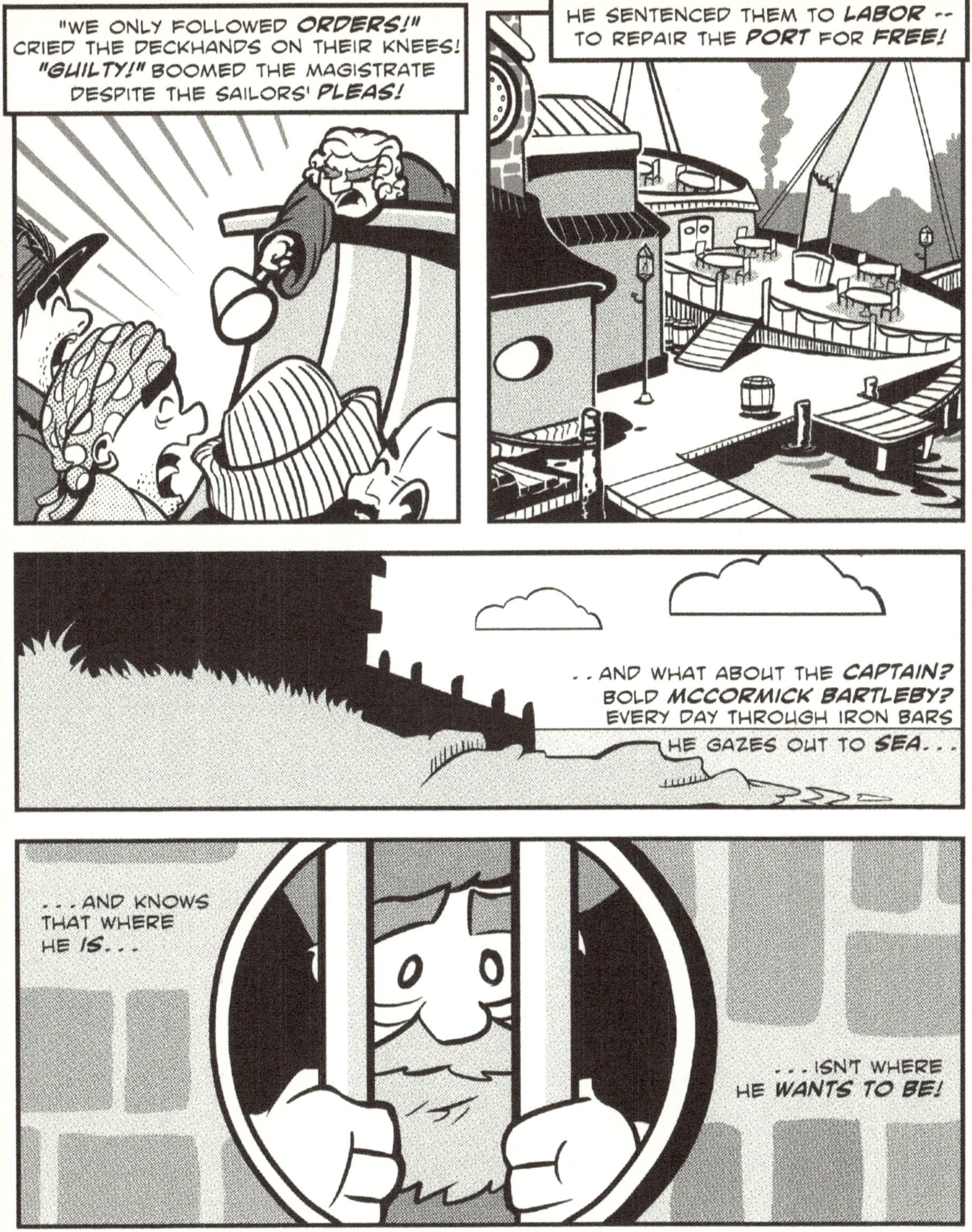
"WE ONLY FOLLOWED ORDERS!" CRIED THE DECKHANDS ON THEIR KNEES! "GUILTY!" BOOMED THE MAGISTRATE DESPITE THE SAILORS' PLEAS!
HE SENTENCED THEM TO LABOR -- TO REPAIR THE PORT FOR FREE!
. . AND WHAT ABOUT THE CAPTAIN? BOLD MCCORMICK BARTLEBY? EVERY DAY THROUGH IRON BARS
HE GAZES OUT TO SEA. . .
. . . AND KNOWS THAT WHERE HE IS. . .
. . . ISN'T WHERE HE WANTS TO BE!

armble: *v.* to wave one's arms in a leisurely fashion

When the Angel Stirred the Waters

by Jonathan Rogers

I have heard the mermaids singing each to each.
I do not think that they will sing to me.
—T.S. Eliot, from "The Love Song of J. Alfred Prufrock"

In the years since Ramona joined the mermaid show, Randall had spent most afternoons beside the whirl hole, drunk. The slow swirl of the water (and also the liquor) eased his troubled mind. His friends were always there, such as they were—drunks and ne'er-do-wells, moochers and cashers of disability checks. Randall had never thought of himself as one of them, but after twenty years, if he wasn't one of them it was hard to say what he might be instead.

The old guard was entirely gone, half of them dead, half gone straight. When Step-and-a-Half drowned, a few of them got religion and never came to the whirl hole again. Among those who left was Randall's best friend Toby, whom he hated. The younger guys were all right, but they knew little of suffering and seemed to think the sandy banks of the whirl hole were their personal pleasure grounds. Some of them even brought girls on the weekends. They rarely left a man to his ruminations.

The sun was already high in the sky when Randall was awakened by the scratch and snuffle of an armadillo rooting through the leaves near his head. Squinting through swollen eyelids, he saw not the pebbled texture of his bedroom ceiling, but the shifting green and brightness of sunlight filtering through the leaves of a live oak. His throbbing head was pillowed on a mound of Spanish moss.

With a groan, Randall raised himself up on an elbow and turned toward the sound of the armadillo, which clattered off into the sparkleberry bushes. Even that much noise felt to Randall like a cheese grater rasping across the inner lining of his skull.

Randall's work uniform, he noticed, was covered with sand and leaf litter, as if he had been wallowing on the ground all night. He had the dim recollection that perhaps he had.

Randall wasn't in the habit of passing out drunk, but the day before had been a hard one. Coming home from third shift at the prison, he drove past Ramona's mother's house, and there in the driveway sat a white Lexus. He drove past again more slowly and saw that the car had a Florida license plate and a window decal of a mermaid seated like a mud-flap girl, knees up and elbows thrown back.

Ramona was in town. Probably with her dentist husband.

Randall had only seen Ramona once since she graduated high school and left Lister for good. He and Toby drove down to Weeki Wachee to watch her in the mermaid show. They sat in the front row, not ten feet from the tank. In her bespangled Lycra tailfin and clamshell bikini top, Ramona was scarcely recognizable as the girl they had known in Lister. She swam with a grace and power that suggested that perhaps the water, as she had always said, truly was her native element. She was a sea nymph, a daughter of Triton. When she drank a Coca-Cola underwater, Randall and Toby leapt to their feet and clapped and hooted wildly.

After the show, Randall barely had the chance to speak to her. Toby had to get back for work, and Ramona's next performance was in fifteen minutes anyway. She spoke politely to them as she sat on the fake rock still wearing her fake tailfin and blinking her fake eyelashes, but it was clear to Randall that she had moved on. How could two boys from Lister expect to hold the attention of a mermaid?

Ramona did come back home for her wedding, easily the biggest the town had ever seen. The dentist paid for it. The five bridesmaids were all mermaids, not Lister girls, and they all wore their tailfins. Randall never understood how they got down the aisle without the use of their feet; he wasn't there to see it. Though he was invited, he couldn't bring himself to go. "It'll give us closure," Toby had said. But Randall didn't want closure. And the fact that Toby did suggested that he didn't love Ramona as much as he claimed to—and not nearly as much as Randall did.

Having turned around for a second look at the Lexus, Randall kept on driving, and not toward home. When Lister Liquors opened that morning, Randall was waiting at the door. When his drinking buddies arrived at the whirl hole that afternoon, he was drunk already.

Now it was Saturday and getting close to noon, and Randall's tongue felt like a whetstone in his mouth. His gorge rose at the sight of the empty whiskey bottle lying beside his knee. He needed water. Indeed, he felt that he would never again drink anything besides water. So on knees and elbows he dragged himself to the water's edge, stopping twice to let his head and stomach settle.

The whirl hole was an artesian well, about twice the size of a public pool and elliptical in shape. Its water was purer even than the tap water in Lister. Randall submerged his whole head and drank by gulps. He came up for air, then plunged his head in again. His slitted eyes opened wide, and he watched the sway of the broad grasses on the sandy bottom. The gentle stir of the water began to soothe the ache in his head, but before it could finish its work he was startled out of his reverie by the approach of something big and dark. He lurched backward onto the sand and was astonished to see the black, knobbed head of an alligator float past the very spot where his own head had been a second earlier, followed by the broad, grooved back of an alligator and the two high ridges of an alligator's tail making a sinuous parallel before meeting in a narrow V at the tip. The great reptile was eight feet long, maybe nine. Not propelling itself, it floated in the rotating current of the whirl hole.

Randall marveled as the prehistoric giant made a slow lap around the ellipse of the pool. It occurred to him that he might be hallucinating. He had, after all, drunk a lot of whiskey. He picked up one of the dozens of cans that littered the bank and flung it at the alligator as it floated past again. It bounced off the armored back with an aluminum ping and lighted in the water, where it was carried along by the same current that carried the undisturbed alligator.

All his life Randall had been coming to the whirl hole, but he had never seen an alligator here, had never even heard of an alligator here. Before the drunks took over, the whirl hole was the best place to swim in Lister. He and Toby swam here as boys—or, rather, they played in the water here, since neither could swim. One would jump from the live oak into the water, and the other would fish him out with a wooden pole they kept on the bank for that very purpose.

When they were older, Randall and Toby watched Ramona swim in the whirl hole, strengthening her strokes and practicing her tricks against the day when she would drive south to audition for the mermaid show. She back-stroked whole ellipses with the current and breast-stroked whole ellipses against the current and treaded water for minutes at a time and raised herself out of the water like one of Esther Williams's synchronized swimmers, keeping her feet together all the while and kicking like a dolphin. She twisted and flipped, as lithe as an otter, smiling and waving at her two-man audience the way the mermaids did at Weeki Wachee—elbow elbow, wrist wrist wrist.

Yes, Randall had seen some wondrous things at the whirl hole. But he had never seen an alligator. Every time it came around, he bounced another can off its hide, as if to convince himself that it wasn't an apparition or a trick of the light. The smiling alligator paid no mind either to Randall or to the cans he threw.

By the time Darrell and Chuck arrived, the first of the whirl hole regulars, a dozen cans floated alongside or behind the alligator, like a fleet of john boats escorting an aircraft carrier. It was on the far side of the pool when the boys shuffled up, and they didn't notice it. Their attention was on Randall.

"There's the old sinner!" Darrell whooped. "Back early, or still here?" The sound of his voice brought Randall's hangover back in its full power.

"How'm I supposed to keep on the straight and narrow when I see my elders and role models getting drunker than a skunk?" Chuck asked. "Contributing to the delinquency of a minor, that's what you been doing, Randall." Neither Darrell nor Chuck were minors, but they were a good fifteen years younger than Randall.

Randall tried to pretend he couldn't hear them, though he winced at every syllable. He just kept watching the alligator, now rounding the last curve and heading into the final stretch.

"I wanted to bundle you up and take you home," Darrell said, "but Chuck said it would be a shame to disturb you. So I piled up that moss for a pillow to make you more comfortable."

"We figured you was safe enough, too passed out to roll into the water," Chuck began, but he stopped short when he saw what Randall was looking at. "Hot-a-mighty-dog!" he shouted, pointing excitedly at the alligator. "Darrell, do you see this?"

Darrell looked where Chuck was pointing. "Somebody throw a log in the whirl hole?" he asked. But as soon as the words were out of his mouth he realized that it wasn't a log. He whistled low and long. "Would you look at that bastard?" he breathed.

Chuck scanned the bank for something to throw at the alligator and found Randall's whiskey bottle. He winged it, but in his excitement he overshot the alligator by a yard. The bottle joined the convoy of cans trailing the alligator, which continued circling, unperturbed.

Randall shoved Chuck. "Stop it," he said. "You're going to hurt it."

"I by God hope I hurt it," Chuck answered. "I don't want to get ate by no alligator."

"If that alligator had a mind to eat anybody," Randall said, "it would have ate me while I was passed out drunk in the sand. It's been floating around in circles since before I woke up, not bothering anybody."

The alligator was only a few feet away from them now. Randall noticed that Darrell had picked up the wooden rescue pole and hoisted it to his shoulder like a harpooner, ready to jab the alligator in the eye when it came a little closer. Randall knocked the pole out of his hands before he could do it.

"Leave my alligator alone," he said.

Chuck snorted. "Your alligator? What, did you bring it from home and put it in the whirl hole?"

"Well, I was the first to see it," Randall said, "and it ain't hurting anybody. I just like watching it."

The three of them had watched the alligator for two more laps and bounced six more beer cans off its hide before Hugh and Walter showed up. "We're watching

Randall's alligator," Darrell announced. "Don't try to hurt it or Randall might knock you down."

Hugh and Walter joined in the alligator-watching and were willing enough to leave the alligator unmolested except for the barrage of aluminum cans every time it passed them.

But Chuck couldn't resist the temptation to run the quarter-mile to the liquor store to tell about the alligator in the whirl hole. From there, word spread quickly throughout the town, where there was little to do on a Saturday afternoon, and by the time a half-hour had passed, it seemed all of Lister had made its way to the whirl hole. Randall grew increasingly agitated as he thwarted the locals' plans to shoot the alligator or lasso the alligator or wrestle the alligator or beat it with sticks. He ran a whole passel of schoolboys out of the live oak, where they were breaking off branches and throwing them at the alligator as it passed beneath them. In no time, the banks of the whirl hole were clear of beer cans; they were all in the water trailing the alligator, which despite its considerable audience was still as self-possessed as ever.

Randall's nerves were already on edge when Toby made his appearance. Toby got right into the festive spirit of things. If anything had ever happened in Lister that was more exciting than an alligator in the whirl hole, Toby didn't remember it. It struck him as the kind of event that could bring people together and rekindle long dormant feelings of brotherly love.

"Randall," he said, extending his right hand, "it's been a while." Randall took his hand, but only because he didn't know what else to do, surprised as he was at his old friend's appearance at the whirl hole, which he had sworn off. Toby had gotten jowly and a little fat since last time Randall had seen him.

"Thought you were too good for the whirl hole," Randall said.

"I'm not too good for the whirl hole," Toby answered, "but the whirl hole was none too good for me, if you know what I mean."

"I don't know what you mean," said Randall, answering Toby's conciliatory smile with a scowl.

Toby dropped Randall's hand, and an awkward silence prevailed in spite of the whooping and carrying on that swirled around them.

"Anyway," said Toby, gesturing toward the alligator, "I didn't want to miss this."

"Hey!" Randall shouted, and at first Toby thought he was shouting at him. But he was pointing past Toby at a woman in a tank top who had an empty gin bottle cocked behind her ear. "Put that down!"

Toby, determined to connect with his old friend, cast about to find something they still had in common. "Ramona said alligators used to get in the tank at Weeki Wachee," he said. " But they wouldn't cancel the show unless the gator was bigger than four foot."

Scanning the crowd for any sign of hostility toward his alligator, Randall acted as if he hadn't heard Toby.

"Can you imagine?" Toby continued. "Those mermaids swimming with alligators! They just push them out of the way and get on with the show." He gestured with his right hand like a running back giving a stiff-arm.

Randall continued to ignore Toby. Walter, overhearing their conversation, shook his head and ran a hand through his greasy hair. "Them mermaids are badass," he observed.

A sneer distorted Randall's face as he glared at Toby. "So now you know more about mermaids than I do?" he said.

"I ain't trying to get sideways with you, Randall," Toby said. "You got no need to take offense.

Randall sniffed and continued his surveillance of the crowd.

Toby kept at it. "Speaking of Ramona, did you know she's in town?"

"Yes," Randall said quietly and without looking at Toby. "I knew that." He kicked at something in the sand. "I reckon you went to see her?"

"I did."

"And her dentist husband?"

"Him too."

"You bowed and scraped to him too, did you?"

"I didn't bow or scrape, Randall. He's not a bad feller. He invited me to go fishing on his boat. In the Gulf."

Randall finally looked at Toby, searching his face. Then he reached back a ropy arm and punched Toby on the eyebrow.

Toby staggered back a step, as much from surprise as from the blow itself. He stared at Randall in mute astonishment, his brow knitted and his mouth open. The dumbfounded look on his face infuriated Randall even further. "You don't know one thing," he growled. He lunged at Toby, grabbed two fistfuls of shirt, and slung Toby to the ground.

The two men kicked and struggled in the sand. The crowd turned its attention from the alligator and formed a circle around the men. For a second or two, nobody spoke, so shocked they were at the sight of two forty-year-old men writhing on the ground like a couple of schoolboys, one paunchy, one wiry. But soon they found their voices, and they whooped and howled and pumped their fists in the air, egging them on to greater deeds of glory.

Randall managed to get on top of Toby. He put both knees on his chest and wrapped his fingers around his throat. "You never loved her," he hissed. "You never suffered."

Toby was a gentler soul than Randall, but he was also bigger; when Randall's fingers began to clinch around his throat, his survival instinct engaged and he easily threw the smaller man. A great shout went up from the onlookers when they saw that Toby was ready to do battle in earnest.

Both men rose to their feet, then they charged toward one another and collided with a fleshy slap and a thud. Randall's foot slipped and the two men fell in a pile near the water's edge. Toby wrapped his arms around Randall as if to subdue him—or perhaps to soothe him the way a mother enfolds a fretful child in her arms. But Randall wouldn't be subdued or soothed either one. He head-butted Toby, stunning him for a moment. He wiggled out of Toby's embrace and climbed on his back, boxing him on the ears. Toby rolled over on his back, crushing Randall under his weight, and the two men rolled over again and then again, and then they found themselves in the whirl hole, where they continued to struggle. They thrashed the water to a froth; the onlookers closest to the water's edge got good and wet from their splashing.

The combatants unclenched and stood facing one another in waist-deep water. Both men put their hands on their knees, trying to catch their breath. Randall still glared at Toby. Then a look of sadness softened his face. "You left me too," he said. "Why did you leave me, Toby?"

Toby shook his head and smiled. "You stupid sumbitch," he said. "Nobody asked you to suffer. You took that on your own self, and it didn't do anybody a lick of good."

Randall's face twisted again into a tight snarl; with the last of his strength, Randall lunged at Toby, pushing him backward into the deep water. Toby grabbed instinctively at Randall, pulling him with him. Now they found themselves in water that was over their heads. Neither man could swim.

Unaware of the danger, the assembled crowd mistook their flailings and splutterings for the awkward gyrations of inexperienced fighters. The townspeople pushed and jostled one another for a better view. Randall and Toby went down once and came up again clutching at one another, unable either to find help or give it. They went down a second time and somehow managed to come up again. This time, Randall could tell that the shouts of the crowd had changed to something more urgent and focused. And when he looked to the right he saw why. The alligator was coming around again—only this time it was not floating lazily but propelling itself forward, its pink, toothy maw open wide.

But then a female form in a green, billowing skirt flashed through the water and intercepted the alligator, giving it a firm shove just behind its front leg, sending it off-course and away from the drowning men. The outstretched hand, Randall noticed, had salon-perfect nails and three shining rings.

With a graceful flip-turn, the woman swam with smooth, powerful strokes back toward the bank. Simultaneously, the end of the rescue pole appeared in front of Randall and Toby. They grabbed hold and let themselves be pulled toward safety.

At the other end of the pole was a man Randall had never seen before. He was silver-haired and deeply tanned with a strong chin and teeth so white and straight that he scarcely looked human. He wore a pink golf shirt and white pants like Randall had seen men wear on television, but never in Lister.

The woman who had saved Randall and Toby from the alligator made it to the water's edge before they did. Still holding the rescue pole with his right hand, the silver-haired man reached out to the woman with his left to help her out of the water.

Dripping on the bank, her green skirt clinging to her legs like a sheath, the woman scarcely acknowledged the wild applause of the onlookers but instead turned toward Randall and Toby, beamed on them a beatific smile, and waved—elbow elbow, wrist wrist wrist.

Her hair was smaller. Her hips were bigger. But there was no mistaking those cheekbones or those blue eyes that turned down at the corners. Her beauty hadn't faded in the years since Randall had seen her last. Rather, it had grown and deepened.

No choice Randall had made in the previous twenty years had prepared him for the stab of joy he felt when Ramona's silver-haired dentist kissed her square on her lovely mouth. For the first time Randall saw Ramona as a woman, and not just a blank screen on which he could project his fantasies of how the world should be, or his darker dramas of self-loathing. She was a woman, and beautiful, and happy, and Randall was glad of it.

Standing knee-deep in the whirl hole, Randall laughed his first real laugh in years, and marveled at what a fool he'd been.

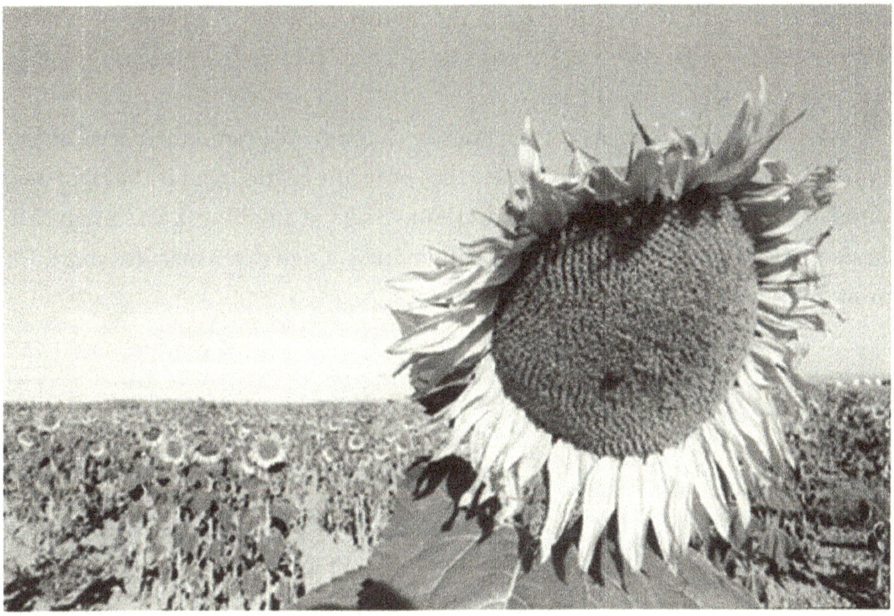

Sunflowers on Swine

by Eric Peters

Two thousand pigs drowned in the sea that afternoon. We watched them racing down the bank in a startled frenzy, as if a legion of demons had overtaken them. We supposed the world was ending, with the reprehensible sounds they made, the squealing chaos, and the filth left in their wake. But the world did not end. For one tormented soul whom we had seen day in and day out, it was beginning anew.

Living among tombs, sleeping with death, long tortured by demons, and driven to paranoia, the old Adam of a man could recall nothing of how he came to be a pariah, nor why life inflicted such cruelty upon him. But seeing a new Adam appear from across the gulf, he wrenched apart the chains that bound him and ran to meet the stranger. Once face to face, the old scar of a man tumbled to his knees begging that ocean of a soul to have mercy.

We flowers cannot explain what we saw that day. We can only marvel at the mystery and wonder of a life not ended, but only just begun. And if the sight and sound of all that bloated, reeking pig death was a sign of anything, it was a sign that the world is as rife with surprise as it is with sadness, a sign that a merciful shore lies on the far side of the sea.

Advent I

by Rebecca Reynolds

I come from people who read rivers instead of books.
They know where the walleye hide
and keep their tomatoes alive in the drought year.

Pappaw courted wild turkeys
with a four-inch piece of round wood.
He carried a loaded pistol to shoot the snakes
and spat his tobacco juice in a line.

On Saturdays his whiskers scratched,
but come Sunday he was smooth as a deacon.
When I kissed him, he smelled sweet
like Aqua Velva and fresh bluegill.

Christmas dinners the men wore white
V-neck T-shirts, with their chest hairs curling at the collars.
We gave one another camouflage jackets,
and long grey utility socks.

We read Luke 2 from that heavy, old Bible
while the children wiggled,
and mostly we were grateful.

Then we sank into old couches and sagging blue recliners,
sticking our bare toes and fingers
through holes in yarn blankets,
sitting close together, making up time
with our arms thrown 'round people
who shared our blood.

Both my grandmothers were artists.
They took classes in Madisonville
and learned the importance of a good bristle brush.
They taught me how to sit before a stretched canvas
lining out wooden barns falling down
or forming the legs of a squirrel.

By Christmas, the walls were full.
There were paintings of daisies,
and three sweet wrens,
(and wooden barns falling down),
and deer standing solemnly in moonlight.

The cedar tree stood a ways from the wood-burning stove.
I pulled the bagworms off of it and threw them in the fire.
That stove was always ten degrees too hot
because Pappaw had known what it meant to be cold.
So we sweated and were thankful when
some great aunt showed up in a fitted tweed jacket,
blasting a line of winter among us.

Mammaw decorated her house
with those big hot bulbs of painted-over glass,
and she used fiberglass angels
that Mom told me not to touch
because they would scratch my eyes.

There was a toilet seat covered in blue foam.
It stuck to your backside and sighed when you sat.
I figured that sort of thing was a comfort to old people.

Mammaw kept her diary in the second bathroom drawer from the right.
I read it once when I was old enough to know better.
I saw how she prayed for me
when nobody was watching but Jesus.

Out in the living room the television made noise and static,
and my people slept before it, not listening,
sometimes waking long enough to comment
on who had grown fat, or thin, or who had grown breasts,
or developed a growth on his neck,
or maintained her bowel movements.

I would sneak out, up to that room
where my dad slept as a boy,
and where I slept summers
with my hair full of sand from the pile.

The four walls were blonde wood paneling,
and there were medals from a track meet,
and a senior picture of my aunt
(who they said looked like me, but didn't).
The blankets smelled like fried potatoes.

I pulled back the thin white curtain
and looked out into the yard where
the world was stripped down to lines.
The trees were calligraphic,
messages I couldn't translate.
And the lights of the coal mine were yellow,
running down a slant into the earth,
while the natural gas pumps genuflected,
working out their mass, even on Christmas Day.
The garden was frozen.
I could tell it would crunch under my shoes.
I looked over it into the heavy, brown sky and
wished to find the Star of Bethlehem.

I watched a good while for something I couldn't name,
then decided to just whisper some lines
I had memorized in school,
though I didn't understand how they fit.

For unto you is born this day a Savior,
who is Christ the Lord.

The Shop of Ghosts

by G. K. Chesterton

Nearly all the best and most precious things in the universe you can get for a halfpenny. I make an exception, of course, of the sun, the moon, the earth, people, stars, thunderstorms, and such trifles. You can get them for nothing. Also I make an exception of another thing, which I am not allowed to mention in this paper, and of which the lowest price is a penny halfpenny. But the general principle will be at once apparent. In the street behind me, for instance, you can now get a ride on an electric tram for a halfpenny. To be on an electric tram is to be on a flying castle in a fairy tale. You can get quite a large number of brightly coloured sweets for a halfpenny. Also you can get the chance of reading this article for a halfpenny; along, of course, with other and irrelevant matter.

But if you want to see what a vast and bewildering array of valuable things you can get at a halfpenny each you should do as I was doing last night. I was gluing my nose against the glass of a very small and dimly lit toy shop in one of the greyest and leanest of the streets of Battersea. But dim as was that square of light, it was filled (as a child once said to me) with all the colours God ever made. Those toys of the poor were like the children who buy them; they were all dirty; but they were all bright. For my part, I think brightness more important than cleanliness; since the first is of the soul, and the second of the body. You must excuse me; I am a democrat; I know I am out of fashion in the modern world.

As I looked at that palace of pigmy wonders, at small green omnibuses, at small blue elephants, at small black dolls, and small red Noah's arks, I must have fallen into some sort of unnatural trance. That lit shop-window became like the brilliantly lit stage when one is watching some highly coloured comedy. I forgot the grey houses and the grimy people behind me as one forgets the dark galleries and the dim crowds at a theatre. It seemed as if the little objects behind the glass were small, not because they were toys, but because they were objects far away. The green omnibus was really a green omnibus, a green Bayswater omnibus, passing across some huge desert on its ordinary way to Bayswater. The blue elephant was no longer blue with paint; he was blue with distance. The black doll was really a negro relieved against passionate tropic foliage in the land where every weed is flaming and only man is black. The red Noah's ark was really the enormous ship of earthly salvation riding on the rain-swollen sea, red in the first morning of hope.

Every one, I suppose, knows such stunning instants of abstraction, such brilliant blanks in the mind. In such moments one can see the face of one's own best friend as an unmeaning pattern of spectacles or moustaches. They are commonly marked by the two signs of the slowness of their growth and the suddenness of their termination. The return to real thinking is often as abrupt as bumping into a man. Very often indeed (in my case) it is bumping into a man. But in any case the awakening is always emphatic and, generally speaking, it is always complete. Now, in this case, I did come back with a shock of sanity to the consciousness that I was, after all, only staring into a dingy little toy-shop; but in some strange way the mental cure did not seem to be final. There was still in my mind an unmanageable something that told me that I had strayed into some odd atmosphere, or that I had already done some odd thing. I felt as if I had worked a miracle or committed a sin. It was as if I had at any rate, stepped across some border in the soul.

To shake off this dangerous and dreamy sense I went into the shop and tried to buy wooden soldiers. The man in the shop was very old and broken, with confused white hair covering his head and half his face, hair so startlingly white that it looked almost artificial. Yet though he was senile and even sick, there was nothing of suffering in his eyes; he looked rather as if he were gradually falling asleep in a not unkindly decay. He gave me the wooden soldiers, but when I put down the money he did not at first seem to see it; then he blinked at it feebly, and then he pushed it feebly away.

"No, no," he said vaguely. "I never have. I never have. We are rather old-fashioned here."

"Not taking money," I replied, "seems to me more like an uncommonly new fashion than an old one."

"I never have," said the old man, blinking and blowing his nose; "I've always given presents. I'm too old to stop."

"Good heavens!" I said. "What can you mean? Why, you might be Father Christmas."

"I am Father Christmas," he said apologetically, and blew his nose again.

The lamps could not have been lighted yet in the street outside. At any rate, I could see nothing against the darkness but the shining shop-window. There were no sounds of steps or voices in the street; I might have strayed into some new and sunless world. But something had cut the chords of common sense, and I could not feel even surprise except sleepily. Something made me say, "You look ill, Father Christmas."

"I am dying," he said.

I did not speak, and it was he who spoke again.

"All the new people have left my shop. I cannot understand it. They seem to object to me on such curious and inconsistent sort of grounds, these scientific men, and these innovators. They say that I give people superstitions and make them too visionary; they say I give people sausages and make them too coarse. They say my heavenly parts are too heavenly; they say my earthly parts are too earthly; I don't know what they want, I'm sure. How can heavenly things be too heavenly, or earthly things too earthly? How can one be too good, or too jolly? I don't understand. But I understand one thing well enough. These modern people are living and I am dead."

"You may be dead," I replied. "You ought to know. But as for what they are doing, do not call it living."

A silence fell suddenly between us which I somehow expected to be unbroken. But it had not fallen for more than a few seconds when, in the utter stillness, I distinctly heard a very rapid step coming nearer and nearer along the street. The next moment a figure flung itself into the shop and stood framed in the doorway. He wore a large white hat tilted back as if in impatience; he had tight black old-fashioned pantaloons, a gaudy old-fashioned stock and waistcoat, and an old fantastic coat. He had large, wide-open, luminous eyes like those of an arresting actor; he had a pale, nervous face, and a fringe of beard. He took in the shop and the old man in a look that seemed literally a flash and uttered the exclamation of a man utterly staggered.

"Good lord!" he cried out; "it can't be you! It isn't you! I came to ask where your grave was."

"I'm not dead yet, Mr. Dickens," said the old gentleman, with a feeble smile; "but I'm dying," he hastened to add reassuringly.

"But, dash it all, you were dying in my time," said Mr. Charles Dickens with animation; "and you don't look a day older."

"I've felt like this for a long time," said Father Christmas.

Mr. Dickens turned his back and put his head out of the door into the darkness.

"Dick," he roared at the top of his voice, "he's still alive."

Another shadow darkened the doorway, and a much larger and more full-blooded gentleman in an enormous periwig came in, fanning his flushed face with a military hat of the cut of Queen Anne. He carried his head well back like a soldier, and his hot face had even a look of arrogance, which was suddenly contradicted by his eyes, which were literally as humble as a dog's. His sword made a great clatter, as if the shop were too small for it.

"Indeed," said Sir Richard Steele, "'tis a most prodigious matter, for the man was dying when I wrote about Sir Roger de Coverley and his Christmas Day."

My senses were growing dimmer and the room darker. It seemed to be filled with newcomers.

"It hath ever been understood," said a burly man, who carried his head humorously and obstinately a little on one side—I think he was Ben Jonson—"It hath ever been understood, consule Jacobo, under our King James and her late Majesty, that such good and hearty customs were fallen sick, and like to pass from the world. This grey beard most surely was no lustier when I knew him than now."

And I also thought I heard a green-clad man, like Robin Hood, say in some mixed Norman French, "But I saw the man dying."

"I have felt like this a long time," said Father Christmas, in his feeble way again.

Mr. Charles Dickens suddenly leant across to him.

"Since when?" he asked. "Since you were born?"

"Yes," said the old man, and sank shaking into a chair. "I have been always dying."

Mr. Dickens took off his hat with a flourish like a man calling a mob to rise.

"I understand it now," he cried, "you will never die."

plodge: *v.* to avoid a hazard laboriously and without haste

Advent II

by Rebecca Reynolds

We flutter around the Gospel
like women with dustpans
nervous that our houses will be caught untidy.
We clasp our pearls behind our necks,
tighten our aprons behind our backs,
and wobble on three-inch peep-toe heels
determined to bring the world to rights,
as if the earth were only cluttered,
as if a careless child
had dropped his school papers
and we might bend to pick them up.

Look again.
Look again at the great hell-wave
that has washed over us.
Every building for mile upon mile
has been broken down.
Every stronghold has come to chaos.
The way is littered with rotting bodies,

grown men walking dazed and naked,
voices lost for their lost women,
women lost, wailing for lost children,
children lost, folded over in grief.

And we are not above but among them,
we who are dressed to the nines,
bleeding and bare,
starved half to death.

We stand high in our poverty
with good intentions
that cannot bring a single damned thing to rights.
Come down from your religion.
Come down from your agitated doings.
Come down from that ladder
where you paint your own thin blood
across the doorframe
hoping that it might suffice.
It will not.

I have met the ends of my strength.
I have seen what I am alone.
It is every rotten thing you have suspected.
Or if you don't believe me,
I will pull back the curtain,
and I will show you everything,
and you will recoil.

So here is my apron.
Here are my shoes.

Take these pearls,
and let me kneel
without pretense
and wait
for tidings of great joy.

writtle: *n.* a puzzling legal order issued by a very small court

Ascension

by Fr. Thomas McKenzie

An isolated town is in trouble. Maybe it's a gang of outlaws. Maybe it's a greedy rancher, or a dictatorial mayor. In any case, bad men are having their way with the townsfolk. More importantly, there's a beautiful woman in town, and they're after her too. She's resisting tyranny—of course she is—while working to help the oppressed.

Then a cowboy rides into town. He's tough. He's quiet. He's got a heart of gold. He's drawn into the conflict. He shoots a bunch of bad people and works his way up to the chief bad guy himself. A showdown ensues—of course it does. The town is saved. The beautiful woman asks the cowboy to stay, but he can't. He has to ride on, back out into the wilderness.

I have always loved Westerns. I will watch any movie that features a cowboy with a six-shooter. I was born and raised in West Texas, and that is partially to blame for this affection. As a boy I would watch an episode of *The Lone Ranger*, and then I'd put on my sheriff's badge, grab my cap guns, and walk out onto the range, ready for adventure.

I'm not alone either. Americans love Westerns. We're fascinated by the myth of the cowboy-hero. But of all the cowboy heroes, my favorite is Captain James Tiberius Kirk. Wait. What? Don't act so surprised. Surely you knew that *Star Trek* was a Western, right? The only difference is that Kirk beamed in with a transporter rather than rode in on a horse.

Let us investigate: Captain Kirk, accompanied by sidekicks, rides down to the lonely planet on his transporter beam. He fights the bad guys, rescues the planet, and leaves the beautiful woman behind. He beams back to his spaceship leaving grateful aliens to stare up at the sky and wonder what life would be like if only Kirk wasn't such a busy hero.

I had another sci-fi cowboy hero when I was a kid. This one I heard about at church. His name was Jesus. The Ascension of Jesus Christ sounds a lot like the Beaming of Captain Kirk. You remember the story. Forty days after the Resurrection, Jesus meets his followers near Bethany. He tells them to return to Jerusalem and wait for the coming of the Holy Sprit. Then he's gone, up into the sky. Luke describes it this way: "He lifted up his hands and blessed them. While he was blessing them, he left them and was taken up into heaven." (Luke 24:50-53, NIV)

Some Christians see the Ascension as the last page of a dime-store novel called *Jesus the Cowboy Hero: Western Adventure*. Earth was in trouble. The land was dominated by sin, the devil, and other "bad men." God's people were trying to hold out and stay strong. Then one day Jesus rode into their midst. He conquered the bad guys, and the people of God, the beautiful "Bride of Christ," were grateful. They wanted him to stay but he couldn't, he had to move on. So they are left staring up into the sky wondering if they will ever see him again.

Of course, most Christians don't literally think that Jesus is a cowboy-hero. But unfortunately, some of our popular theology is so corrupt that we've essentially made him into one. We've created a cowboy god, a hero who cared enough to come down and save us from sin, but didn't care enough to stick around. He left us tickets for the 3:10 to heaven, but staying in town to help rebuild after the showdown wasn't of much interest to him, and off he rode, a beam of light into the sunset.

That cheap dime-store novel is a lie. The God of the Bible stands in stark contrast to that irrelevant god. Unlike the cowboy who rides off when the showdown is over, the Ascended Christ is now more invested in his Creation than ever.

It was an amazing thing for the non-corporeal God, a being who is not made of anything, to create everything. It was an act of incomprehensible humility for God to become a part of his creation by being made man. It was the greatest act of love imaginable for the God-man to die an insurgent's death, to descend to the dead, and then to rise again to eternal life. It was absolutely inconceivable that this God-man would then take his whole self back into the throne room of his Father. One of the great mysteries of the universe is that Jesus Christ, who is fully God and fully man, now reigns forever in his corporeal body. When Jesus ascended he didn't slither out of his skin, leaving the human part behind. God became a man and now that man is God. For God so loved his Creation (John 3:16), that he has now made himself a part of his Creation forever.

When Jesus was resurrected he appeared to his disciples in a perfect, eternal body, eating and drinking, but also walking through walls. Scripture says that when he ascended he *sat down* at the right hand of God (Ephesians 1:20). Because Jesus is still flesh, he must be in some sort of physical location. But at the same time, he *is* God and sits at the right hand *of* the Father. Where is the "right hand"? Where is God? Everywhere. Christ is both present in a single place and also present everywhere. How? I have no idea. What I do know is that Christ is everywhere available, everywhere loving, everywhere knowable.

But "sitting at the right hand of the Father" is not simply about location; it's about power. Jesus' ascension is his enthronement. Paul writes: "[God] raised Christ from the dead and seated him at his right hand in the heavenly realms, far above all rule and authority, power and dominion, and every name that is invoked, not only in the present age but also in the one to come. And God placed all things under his feet and appointed him to be head over everything for the church, which is his body, the fullness of him who fills everything in every way" (Ephesians 1:20-23 NIV). Christ is the King who fills, with his own self, all that he has made. As Abraham Kuyper said. "There is not a square inch in the whole domain of our human existence over which Christ, who is Sovereign over all, does not cry, 'Mine!'"

The Ascension fundamentally changed the relationships between God, humanity, and the created order. Kirk comes and goes in fifty minutes. Not so with

Christ. The great Church Father St. John Chrysostom pointed out that the same Father who once said to flesh and blood, "you are dust, and to dust you shall return," now looks at the flesh and blood of his Son and says, "sit at my right hand." Jesus' story is the opening and closing chapter of the tale of us all. We were dust. Now we're flesh. We will fall again to dust, but we will be raised to a greater flesh than we can now imagine.

Chrysostom goes on to say that "we who were unworthy of earthly dominion have been raised to the Kingdom on high, have ascended higher than heaven, have come to occupy the King's throne, and the same nature from which the angels guarded Paradise, stopped not until it ascended to the throne of the Lord." God has become Man so that humanity can now be welcomed into the divine life. Creation is already redeemed and awaits its coming restoration.

The Ascension is divine proof that the world matters. This world—the world of cowboys and townsfolk, bad men and heroes—matters. If it did not, why would Christ fill it? Why would he reign over it? Why would he love it? Why would the Father accept the Created onto his own throne?

Because the Ascension changed the world, it must also change the way we understand the world. The Ascension is like a new and better eyeglass prescription. When we look through it, we see what we have always seen; but we see it more clearly. This is especially true of our relationship to Creation.

Many years ago, I moved from Pittsburgh to San Antonio, and during that time I had to live apart from my wife for a couple of months. I lived in an apartment with a month-to-month lease while I looked for a more permanent home. It was an old and dirty unit with broken appliances and dated wallpaper. I had several framed pieces of art with me, but I never hung any of them on the walls. I tried to ignore the walls and the faulty appliances. I never fixed the broken toilet in the second bathroom. Why not? Because it was a transitional place. I didn't care about it.

Many Christians, lacking an understanding of the Ascension (as well as the Creation, Incarnation, and Second Coming) treat this world like I treated that apartment. While it's true that we are sojourners (Hebrews 11:16), the Ascension must reframe our thinking. We are called to live here like my wife and I lived at our more permanent place in Texas. We bought furniture. We painted a room. We kept the place in good repair. We hung up our pictures.

The Ascension shows us that the created world matters because it's filled with Christ. As Christ's brothers and sisters, we are called upon to care for creation. The curse is rolling back, and Adam's children are called once again to care for God's garden. When some company wants to strip the land with no regard for our grandchildren, it should be the Church that rises up in opposition. When it comes to making decisions about how we consume the earth's resources, it should be Christians who are most willing to sacrifice our convenience. Christians should be known for the creative ways in which we protect and restore the world we inhabit here and now.

We who bear the image of Christ should be leading the way in caring for our own physical bodies while also showing concern for the health of all people. Medicine, exercise, biology, nutrition, and a whole host of other disciplines are meant to bring glory to Christ. Eating disorders, drunkenness, and sexual immorality are symptoms of a population that has not been formed in the beauty of the Ascended Christ.

The Creation matters, and so does co-creation. By "co-creation" I mean our participation with God in bringing order, truth, and beauty out of chaos. All of Creation is now under the gracious dominion of Christ. When we co-create with him, our work becomes part of his glorious kingdom. Everything from our painting and songwriting to our baking and childrearing finds eternal significance at the Father's right hand. The Ascension proclaims the validity of our work, our creativity, and the joys of this world.

The Ascension challenges us to rethink our cowboy mythology, our Captain Kirk worldview. Our stories, especially our fiction, should point to the Truth. The Hero of the universe is fully invested in building up his people, in loving his children, and in ruling all aspects of our lives. He hasn't ridden off into the sunset. He hasn't beamed back into the heavens. He's moved in, and he's done it in the biggest way we can imagine. When we tell our tales, are we representing this kind of heroism? When we consider the narratives of our own lives, what is it that we see as heroic? Is it the full engagement with, and care for, our communities, our families, and even our possessions? It should be.

All of us are storytellers, whether we have a large audience, or a small circle of family and friends, or even if we are simply whispering to ourselves. Some of us, still dusty from a day out on the range, still tell our tales by the campfire. By the grace of God, maybe we can tell true stories. Maybe we can reject isolation and self-sufficiency. Maybe we can know ourselves as fully accepted children of God, people whose work has eternal significance and whose true value is a gift of pure mercy. We're all cowboys to some extent, but maybe it's time we learned to be cowboys who stick around.

Song of Experience

by Rebecca Reynolds

The Lord is my shepherd,
And yet, I want.

He maketh me to lie down
in long, sad years of breaking.

He leadeth me beside
hostile waters
roiling with serpents,
Bible salesmen,
charlatans,
Napoleons,
Judases,
and the evangelists of consumption.

I bleed into that river,
and every hateful, hungry thing
grows wild with want.

Yea, I walk through the valley
of a silence I cannot decipher.
Instead, I brew the tea for supper,
taking care not to let the grinds
break through.

Thy rod and Thy staff
are fearsome to me,
for this morning I lifted
my hands to the heavens and shouted,
"My God! My God,
Why have you forsaken me
to panic,
to fury,
to loneliness,
to injustice,
to betrayal,
to longing,
to failure?"

The hem of holiness flutters,
caught a half-second in the late-April wind.

Has He not made the whole loud world
sing every moment of its turning:

"Glory! Glory! Glory!"
from the tree lights,

"Glory! Glory! Glory!"
from the thousand-throated skies,

"Glory! Glory! Glory!"
Even the rocks cry out with all creation,
until the brightness of their praise rips the sky in half
and throws me, face to the earth,
in a blast

that smooths my fibers
so that I listen,
relinquishing.
"Thou art with me."

frogurt: *n.* dessert made from the milk of a lactating amphibian

Song of Resonance
by Rebecca Reynolds

The Lord is my shepherd.

I am made calm
by the strong turn of His fingers
around the staff that collects me
into His company.

For I am the nervous sort,
bothered and bolting.

His hands have grown thick and brown
from our long, shared days of summer.

This morning I nudged the tip of my nose
against His wrist three times,
leaned the weight of my body against His leg,
hoping that He might lower His forehead
to press it against mine
and whisper anything at all.

His voice is beautiful.
I have heard it rise lung-full and light
as a father laughing over his first-born.
I have heard Him
as a man singing, walking in full stride
over Miller's Ridge.

His hands are warm.
The lines of their wear
are inscribed with secret things,
though I have read my name
in their valleys.

There was frost on the pasture in that first hour.
The maiden sun strained to climb
against the gravity of Earth.
She shook her hair-fire to dry
upon the glass cathedral.

My feet were cold from walking in the wet night grass,
but the Lord is my Shepherd.
The Lord is my Shepherd.
I shall not want forever.

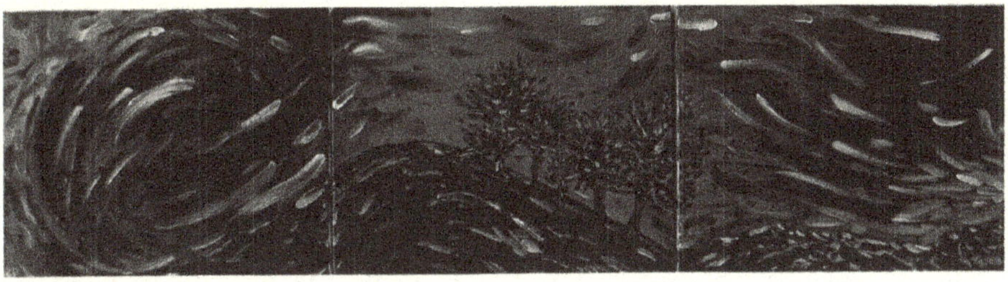

Origins: Fending off the Sadness

by Eric Peters

The artist's act of creating, even on his most godless day, is inherently the creation story retold. But though the artist pronounces his work good, neither his shadows nor his doubts will leave him in peace.

The artist yearns for beginnings, longs to recapture the original moment. He designs to eradicate the darkness by introducing light. The artist is a figure in storm, straining to hear melody amid chaos, very much aware of and susceptible to pain and rejection. If he survives the creative act, the artist may walk away, but never without a limp.

Creating is my way of fending off the sadness. When I paint a canvas, I am wringing the throat of darkness, forcing its movement, coloring the vacuum of shadows, answering the melancholy with color of my own. When working with castoff slabs of old, dingy wood, I am repurposing the original atoms of creation and lending them a particle of myself. By reclaiming lost, unwanted, unnoticed debris, by wiping away the grime of unwelcome memory, and by chipping and scraping away obscuring layers of paint, I am reintroducing the refashioned work into the living fold. When I mow a lawn, I am laboring over something unkempt, and I wrestle it, toil over it, to make it lovely again. By revering the meek, undistinguished objects and scenes of earth, the artist recaptures a grain of the original garden—that place where the soul first felt its worth. The artist sings a song over his subjects' lives of unrealized possibility. He grieves over their lifeless carcasses, prays for resurrection, and, by necessity, dies a little himself. Not all death is to be avoided.

The artist humbles himself before the blank space, prepares his medium, and then asks of them, "What do you wish to be?" By such expression, the artist, wittingly or unwittingly, places himself before the Holy of Holies and pleads, "Your will be done, not mine." And then, in submission, the artist shreds the darkness, repurposing it for good. We are, after all, replicators seeking to aid the blind in seeing their own color of origin. By engaging his heart and hands, the artist stares into the implacable sadness and yanks the light up from the depths. The original garden abounded with light, variety, and beauty, and in his heart the artist clings to his own shimmering point of origin, holding out open hands to receive the alms of light and life, hoping and believing that the light is enough.

M.

Contributors

Sarah Clarkson is the author of *Read for the Heart*, a guide to a healthy reading life for families, and *Journeys of Faithfulness*, stories of life and faith for young Christian women. She hails from the dappled foothills of Colorado and plans to write at least one great novel before she dies. In the meantime, she studies literature and writes about the wondrous world of children's stories. *(www.ThoroughlyAlive.com)*

Zach Franzen is an illustrator who lives with his wife and infant daughter in Greenville, South Carolina. He enjoys tea and baby smiles and is a frequent conspirator at the Story Warren website *(www.StoryWarren.com)*. The illustrations he contributed to this volume were inked entirely with tea (we told you he enjoyed it). He drank the remainder of the cup, and now we'll never know what might have become of it.

Lanier Ivester is a "Southern Lady," in the best and most classical sense, and a gifted writer, in the most articulate and literal sense. She also hand-binds books and lives on a farm with peacocks, bees, sheep, and the governor of Ohio's leg. She and her husband have been known to spend their vacation time in old black-and-white movies. *(www.LaniersBooks.com)*

Jonny Jimison, also known as "that one guy who draws comics," is one guy who draws comics. He lives in Jacksonville, Florida, where he is a freelance illustrator and a builder of Lego spaceships. *(www.JonnyJimison.com)*

Thomas McKenzie is the inimitable host of the One Minute Review and the pastor of Church of the Redeemer in Nashville, Tennessee. Also, he has samurai swords and wears a skull ring. We highly recommend this priest. *(www.OneMinuteReview.com)*

Jeffrey Overstreet is the author of The Auralia Thread series of novels, and a "memoir of dangerous moviegoing"—*Through a Screen Darkly*. He's a film reviewer, a creative writing instructor, a magazine editor, a speaker, a blogger, and a member of the Chrysostom Society. He's currently writing a new novel and preparing himself for a future in which he teaches high school and college students about the Muppets (and possibly writing, and cinema, and art, and faith).

Eric Peters is a singer-songwriter who has recorded six solo albums including *Chrome* and *Birds of Relocation*. He's also a painter, a photographer, a curmudgeon, a lawn connoisseur, and a hopeless bibliophile. The works printed herein are from his forthcoming project, *The Far Side of the Sea*, which is, regrettably, not about pirates. *(www.EricPeters.net)*

A. S. Peterson is the author of the Revolutionary War novels *The Fiddler's Gun* and *Fiddler's Green*. He's also the managing editor of Rabbit Room Press and is a nefarious puppeteer who lurks in the shadows, pulling strings, planning Hutchmoots, plotting books, and conspiring to sail away and have bloody adventures.

Andrew Peterson is the proprietor of the Rabbit Room and the singer-songwriter of more than ten albums including *Light for the Lost Boy*, *Counting Stars*, and *Behold the Lamb of God: The True Tall Tale of the Coming of Christ.* He is also the author of the Christy award-winning Wingfeather Saga and is hard at work writing the fourth book, *The Warden and the Wolf King. (www.Andrew-Peterson.com)*

Russ Ramsey is the author of *Behold the Lamb of God: An Advent Narrative.* He is a pastor at Midtown Fellowship in Nashville, Tennessee, and he remains bravely unapologetic in his appreciation of baseball, floating tremolo systems, big hair, Vanderbilt surgeons, and Dutch painters.

Rebecca Reynolds teaches philosophy and rhetoric at a classical school in eastern Tennessee. She's also the lyricist behind Ron Block's latest album *Walking Song*, and is a leading contender in the race to win Facebook.

Jonathan Rogers is the author of seven books including as the Wilderking Trilogy, *The Charlatan's Boy*, and *The Terrible Speed of Mercy*. After another notably painful delivery, he is also the proud father of exactly two short stories. No alligators were harmed in the creation of either of these tales. *(www.Jonathan-Rogers.com)*

S. D. Smith exists at the lonely crossroads of strange and wise, and is the proprietor of the Story Warren website. He claims that P. G. Wodehouse is his great uncle on his mother's side, but we don't believe him. *(www.StoryWarren.com)*

Jennifer Trafton is the author of *The Rise and Fall of Mount Majestic*, a nominee for the 2012 Volunteer State Book Award. She teaches creative writing to kids, is hard at work on her next book, and would love nothing more than to live on a sailboat with a dancing giraffe. *(www.JenniferTrafton.com)*

Walter Wangerin, Jr. is the National Book Award-winning author of *The Book of the Dun Cow*, *Ragman & Other Cries of Faith*, *Letters from the Land of Cancer*, and many other fine books that we haven't the space to list here. He is also well-known for blowing minds as the keynote speaker at Hutchmoot 2010. *(www.WaltWangerinJr.org)*

e collibus montes

RABBIT ROOM

PRESS

The
RABBIT ROOM

www.RabbitRoom.com

Also available:

The Molehill, Vol. 1

Subjects with Objects
by DKM and Jonathan Richter

Real Love for Real Life
by Andi Ashworth

Monster in the Hollows
by Andrew Peterson

Behold the Lamb of God
by Russ Ramsey

The Cymbal Crashing Clouds
by Ben Shive

The Fiddler's Gun and Fiddler's Green
by A. S. Peterson